RESIST
SURVIVING THE SLIDE TO AUTOCRACY

BARRETT COLE

Disclaimer

The information provided in this book is for informational and educational purposes only. It is designed to provide accurate and authoritative insights into the subject matter covered. However, it is not intended as, nor should it be relied upon as, legal, financial, psychological, or other professional advice. While the author and publisher have made every effort to ensure the accuracy of the information contained within, no representations or warranties are made with respect to the completeness, reliability, or accuracy of the content. The advice and strategies discussed may not be suitable for every individual or situation, especially given the dynamic nature of political and economic environments. Readers are encouraged to consult with qualified professionals in the fields of law, finance, digital security, or mental health as needed. Liability Disclaimer: By reading this book, you acknowledge that the author and publisher are not liable for any loss, harm, or injury—financial, physical, or otherwise—that may arise from following any advice or strategies presented. This includes, but is not limited to, economic losses, personal injury, or legal issues resulting from actions taken based on the information in this book. Use the content at your own discretion and risk. This book does not endorse or advocate any illegal activities or actions that may contravene the laws of your country or region. The content is intended solely to inform and empower readers to navigate challenging circumstances responsibly. If you have concerns about your specific situation, please seek professional advice from a qualified expert. The author and publisher expressly disclaim any liability related to actions taken or not taken based on the contents of this book.

*For the ones willing to step into
the breach when liberty is at risk*

Table of Contents

Chapter 1
A New World Order – Adjusting to Life Under the Big, Not-So-Friendly Government

Well $#!%, so that happened. You're probably reading this book because you're watching the news, noticing some…dramatic shifts in how things are run, and you're wondering: How do I keep my job, my sanity, and maybe even my conscience while navigating this? If you're feeling like society's pendulum is swinging from democracy toward something a little more Orwellian, you're not alone.

But before we start packing the moving van for some other less Gulag-happy country, remember: humans have been living under all kinds of government systems for thousands of years. From emperors to autocrats, people have not only survived but often thrived in ways that upheld their values, communities, and individual integrity. This book isn't about preparing to hide—it's about learning to operate within the system, strategically and effectively, without losing your sense of self. And maybe a little bit about making some "good trouble" near the end.

Welcome to the New Reality

Let's start by acknowledging the shifts we're seeing. For many of us, this isn't the reality we expected: Rights and freedoms that felt foundational suddenly seem conditional. To some, it's unsettling; to others, it's infuriating. Whatever your political stance, the reality is that as power centralizes, those on the margins—often regular, everyday folks—must adapt.

So, the first rule of thumb here? Separate the real landscape from the noise. Yes, there's a lot of drama, but beneath it lies a system with its own rules and order. Figuring out the structure, the real power players, and the areas of stability within the system will help you keep your head down and remain effective without getting swept up in every political wave.

Hallmark Signs of an Autocratic Shift

When a democracy begins to slide toward autocracy, certain signs are almost always visible. Knowing what to look for can help you prepare, stay informed, and make thoughtful choices about how to navigate the environment. Here are some common indicators that a government is tightening its control:

Shifts in Public Messaging: Emphasis on National Security and Traditional Values

Autocratic regimes often invoke the need for "security" and "preservation of values" as reasons for their policies. You might notice increased rhetoric around national strength, stability, and traditional or family values. There may be calls to "protect" society from perceived threats—often vaguely defined but meant to evoke fear and justify restrictive measures. This messaging isn't always aggressive; it can sound patriotic and comforting, but it signals a shift toward controlling public sentiment and defining acceptable behavior or beliefs.

Restrictions on Media and Speech: Greater Control Over Information Channels

Autocracies know that controlling the narrative is essential. As power consolidates, independent journalism, open debate, and free expression become targets. Look for subtle changes, like more frequent government "guidance" to media outlets, higher barriers to broadcasting licenses, or vague restrictions against spreading "false information." You might notice that certain topics are no longer covered in the news or that journalists face pressure to self-censor. Social media platforms may be subject to new regulations or outright suppression to prevent criticism from reaching a wide audience.

Increased Surveillance and Censorship: Both in Public and Online

Autocratic governments often justify increased surveillance as a measure to ensure safety and order. Cameras in public spaces may become more prevalent, and online activity may be subject to greater monitoring. New laws might require tech companies to provide user data or block certain types of content. While this may initially target "threats to security," it often broadens to monitor average citizens. If you're noticing that some sites are suddenly inaccessible or that people are more cautious about what they post or say, it's a sign that censorship is taking hold.

Recognizing these early signs of an autocratic shift can feel daunting, but it's your first step toward navigating the realities they bring. Once you know what to look for, you can start working within the system—not as a passive bystander, but as someone who's grounded, informed, and ready to move strategically. That's where "Knowing the New Rules" comes in, offering insights into the evolving landscape and how to operate within it with clarity and purpose.

Step 1: Knowing the New Rules (or Lack Thereof)

When political systems shift, the rules you once thought unchangeable can suddenly transform. Laws, norms, and protections you trusted might weaken, while new priorities and ideologies take their place. It may feel chaotic, but there's order to even the most authoritarian systems. Here's how to get familiar with the new lay of the land:

1. Identify Power Players and Influence Lines

Not every government agency or organization will function the same way it did before, and not all institutions will carry the same weight. Which agencies are being prioritized? Who has direct lines to those in power? Understanding where the power lies—where influence is concentrated—helps you avoid areas of risk and allows you to work within the system while staying strategic.

2. Learn to Spot "Code Words" and Subtext

As we know from history, certain words or phrases signal significant shifts. Leaders may use terms like "reform," "security," or "safety" to disguise sweeping changes. Learn to read between the lines. Language that seems innocuous might actually signal a major policy shift, so tuning into this subtext will keep you informed.

3. Know Your "Safe Zones"

Even in restrictive environments, there are stable areas. Certain communities, states, or organizations may continue operating independently or neutrally. Identifying these safe zones and the people who frequent them gives you places of stability in an otherwise unstable environment.

Autocratic vs. Democratic Policies: Practical Impacts on Business

Understanding the key differences between democratic and autocratic policies can help business leaders anticipate shifts in the regulatory and economic landscape, particularly as governments move toward more centralized control. Here's a breakdown of how these differences manifest in real-world business operations.

Regulatory Changes: Control and Influence over Industries

In democratic settings, regulations are often developed through checks and balances, public debate, and input from multiple stakeholders. These policies aim to create a fair playing field for businesses, protect consumer rights, and stimulate market competition. Companies generally have a predictable regulatory environment, which allows for strategic long-term planning.

In contrast, autocratic regimes tend to increase direct control over industries, often imposing sudden regulatory changes. Autocratic governments might favor state-controlled enterprises or closely monitor private companies to ensure alignment with government agendas. Financial regulations may shift overnight, and sectors such as energy, technology, and media may face more intense oversight or restrictions. While this can bring temporary stability for the favored sectors, it creates challenges for businesses unaligned with state goals, potentially limiting growth or driving out smaller competitors.

Impact on Business: Businesses under autocratic policies must be agile, ready to adapt to regulatory shifts with little notice. Financial planning may need more conservative cash reserves, as new regulations or licensing requirements can arise unexpectedly, impacting cash flow and operational freedom. Companies may also find themselves needing to engage more directly with government officials to stay ahead of regulatory changes and maintain good standing.

Shift from Market-Driven to State-Driven Initiatives

Democratic economies typically encourage competition and innovation through market-driven initiatives, where supply and demand dictate market dynamics. Private companies thrive on their ability to pivot, innovate, and respond to consumer needs without excessive government interference. Subsidies, if applied, usually focus on fostering innovation and environmental or public good advancements.

In an autocratic shift, however, the focus often moves from market-driven to state-driven initiatives. Governments may prop up certain sectors through subsidies or establish monopolies in areas deemed strategically important, like defense, technology, or agriculture. This often means that the state has greater influence over pricing, distribution, and resources within these favored sectors. Market competition is discouraged, and private businesses may be pressured to partner with state-owned enterprises or adhere to government-dictated priorities.

Impact on Business: Companies operating in autocratic environments might need to adjust their focus to align with state preferences. Private businesses may be limited in their ability to compete with state-backed companies or even face forced collaboration. Businesses not in favored industries may struggle to access financing, or they might encounter barriers if they are seen as competing with state interests. For those in aligned sectors, there can be opportunities for growth, but these often come with heavy government oversight and limited autonomy.

Impact on Workplace Culture and Compliance

In democracies, workplace culture often reflects values of open dialogue, diversity, and employee rights, with a focus on fostering innovation and productivity. Compliance requirements tend to be more about safety, transparency, and fairness, enabling companies to operate with a degree of independence within a framework of established rules.

In autocracies, however, workplace culture can shift under the weight of increasing government oversight and imposed loyalty to state values. Compliance becomes not only about meeting industry standards but also about adhering to state-imposed ideologies or policies. For example, businesses may face mandatory "patriotic" education programs, loyalty oaths, or quotas that reflect government preferences. Employees and management alike may feel pressured to conform to these expectations, and any perceived dissent can lead to fines, closures, or worse.

Impact on Business: Compliance becomes a balancing act between maintaining operational standards and meeting political expectations. HR policies may need to adapt, potentially prioritizing ideological alignment over merit in hiring and promotions. Maintaining a positive public image can require adopting state-favored values in branding, community involvement, and even in employee activities. Noncompliance can bring severe penalties, so businesses must stay informed on shifting political norms and adapt their workplace culture accordingly to avoid repercussions.

Summing Up the Differences

While democratic policies offer a stable environment for business planning, innovation, and fair competition, autocratic policies create a dynamic landscape where adaptability, strategic alignment with state goals, and an understanding of government priorities become essential. By recognizing these distinctions, businesses can proactively adjust their strategies and operate successfully within autocratic frameworks, even as they balance growth with compliance in a high-stakes environment.

Step 2: Adapting to the Culture Shift (Without Losing Your Mind)

Living under an increasingly authoritarian regime doesn't mean you have to change who you are or start waving flags you don't believe in. But it does mean navigating a changing landscape with caution, adaptability, and an eye on your future. Think of it as "strategic silence"—not as an act of suppression, but as a way to protect yourself and make space to pursue your goals, even if the environment around you feels restrictive. Here's how to work within this shifting cultural reality without losing yourself along the way.

Work Within the System

You don't need to endorse or support every policy or directive that comes your way, but choosing not to voice your disagreement with every issue is a form of smart self-preservation. Going along to get along isn't about compromising your principles—it's about conserving your energy for moments where your actions can actually make a difference. Think of it as picking your battles and recognizing that sometimes staying in the game is more impactful than taking yourself out of it entirely.

Practical Tips:

- Choose Your Words Wisely: In environments where loyalty or conformity are rewarded, consider if your opinion on a given issue will truly make a difference. If not, silence may serve you better. Save your voice for issues where you can take a meaningful stand or when discretion won't backfire.

- Focus on Actions, Not Statements: You can still work toward positive change within your sphere of influence, even if it's in subtle ways. Channeling your energy into local, tangible impact might be more effective than public criticism.

The Power of Observation

Observation is your best asset in a landscape that demands constant adaptation. Watch and listen. Notice what's happening in your workplace, social circles, and community. Who's getting ahead, who's struggling, and who's being sidelined? Understanding the power dynamics around you is critical. As public loyalty becomes more important, observing shifts in tone, influence, and behavior can give you a roadmap to navigate without unnecessary risk.

Practical Tips:

- Stay Informed Quietly: Read between the lines in public statements and observe how people respond. What's celebrated, and what's overlooked? This information helps you stay ahead of potential shifts.

- Time Your Voice Carefully: Being outspoken at the wrong moment can be costly. When everyone else is retreating or censoring themselves, it might be wise to do the same. But if you see an opportunity to express your perspective in a way that won't backfire, consider that carefully.

Engage Selectively

There will likely be social or professional events and discussions that don't align with your values or beliefs, but attending these without full engagement can still serve your goals. Maintaining your standing in your workplace or community doesn't have to mean endorsing every word or idea—it can simply mean being present. Strategic engagement allows you to navigate these moments while holding onto your integrity.

Practical Tips:

- "Smile and Nod" Diplomacy: Sometimes, listening and nodding is all that's needed. It signals participation without endorsing.

- Identify Your "Red Lines": Determine which values or issues you can't compromise on, and know where you're willing to draw a boundary. This helps you stay true to your core beliefs while strategically navigating discussions and events that don't align with your views.

Scenario Planning for Businesses and Careers

In an unpredictable environment, having contingency plans isn't just prudent—it's essential.

Consider different scenarios that might arise, such as further tightening of regulations, shifting industry focus, or potential economic fallout. Having alternate paths mapped out allows you to pivot quickly if the situation requires it.

Practical Tips for Planning:

- Alternative Income Streams: Think about building income streams outside of your primary career. Freelance work, online courses, or consulting can provide financial cushion if regulations in your main industry become restrictive.

- Invest in Skill-Building: Consider skill sets that are valuable across industries. Skills like digital literacy, adaptability, or project management can make you more marketable, regardless of policy changes or industry shifts.

- Stay Flexible in Business Practices: For entrepreneurs, focus on resilience by diversifying revenue streams, reducing overhead, and maintaining adaptability. For employees, keep an eye out for roles or departments that are less vulnerable to state influence or political shifts.

Building a Resilient Network

When political and social landscapes change, having a resilient network can be a critical advantage. Networking isn't just about career growth—it's about future-proofing your stability.

Knowing people in various sectors and industries can give you alternative options if the environment continues to change.

Practical Tips for Building a Resilient Network:

- Seek Out Like-Minded Individuals: Even in restrictive environments, you'll find others who share your values. Forming a network of discreet allies who support each other professionally or personally can make a huge difference.

- Cultivate Diverse Connections: Aim to connect with people across a range of fields. Diversity in your network helps you adapt by giving you a variety of perspectives and resources.

- Nurture Professional Relationships Carefully: Keep interactions professional and be cautious of venting frustrations in work or semi-public spaces. A carefully maintained network helps you gain insight into industry trends without compromising yourself.

Navigating the New Normal: Summary

By following these strategies, you can maintain a balance between staying true to yourself and adapting to the cultural shifts around you. Each of these techniques—strategic silence, selective engagement, contingency planning, and resilient networking—allows you to face this new reality without sacrificing your integrity or mental well-being.

Living in a world that values conformity over individualism can be draining, but with the right mindset and strategies, you can carve out a life that respects both your goals and your values. Embrace flexibility, strengthen your support system, and approach the shifting landscape with a sense of practicality. You may not be able to change the world overnight, but you can stay grounded, prepared, and ready to adapt to whatever comes your way.

Step 3: Holding onto Your Values (Without Attracting Attention)

During times of political change, holding onto your values is your compass. But how do you keep them intact without painting a target on your back? Historically, those who succeed under autocratic rule tend to master the art of quiet resilience.

Define Your Non-Negotiables

Write down your non-negotiables—the values or principles that are essential to you. Knowing these in advance gives you something solid to hold onto, even if you feel like you're compromising elsewhere. This list of principles is what will keep you grounded as you navigate each new situation.

Practice "Controlled Transparency"

Be strategic about what you share and with whom. This doesn't mean hiding who you are; it's about conserving energy and expressing yourself in a way that minimizes friction. You can be authentic while being mindful of your words and timing, which will serve you well in the long run.

Keep Perspective

Sometimes, the best way to hold onto your values is to understand that societies go through cycles, and you're not alone in feeling like the world is shifting. Staying connected to your purpose and long-term goals will keep you grounded even when things feel uncertain.

Step 4: Building Quiet Alliances

Autocratic systems often function by creating division and isolation—keeping people separate and distrustful so that organizing is harder. But building alliances quietly is not only possible; it's often essential.

Find Like-Minded People

They're out there. Whether it's a co-worker, a neighbor, or a local organization that feels the same way, building a network of like-minded people doesn't require grand gestures. Small signs of support or shared understanding go a long way.

Support the Helpers

In challenging times, there are always individuals who work quietly for the good of others. Maybe it's a local doctor, lawyer, or teacher who offers support without fanfare. Notice these helpers and, when possible, lend them your quiet support.

Silent Acts of Support

Supporting others doesn't always require loud declarations. Simple actions—showing up, helping out, listening—are powerful in their own way. By quietly reinforcing these alliances, you create a network of solidarity that doesn't need public acknowledgment to be effective.

The Long Game: Patience, Perspective, and Staying Ready

So, as you head into the next chapters, carry this mindset with you: You're allowed to be concerned— your fear is justified. But it's what you do with that fear that matters. Recognize the signs, stay informed, and hold onto the knowledge that you are far from alone. Thousands of people, in this era and before, have faced similar challenges and found ways to thrive without sacrificing their values. As unsettling as this period may be, remember that change is a constant in human history. Autocratic swings, too, are part of cycles, and resilience often lies in patience, perspective, and a sense of humor. If anything, this period will teach us to stay flexible, keep a broad perspective, and cultivate a grounded response to shifting tides.

In the chapters ahead, we'll get into specific strategies for staying financially secure, maintaining mental well-being, and building practical resilience. This book is about thriving on your terms— about holding onto what makes you, you, no matter what shifts around you, even when the system seems to be doing everything but supporting you.

Chapter 2
Playing the Game Without Compromise

So, here you are, navigating a system that feels like it was designed for you to trip up, comply, or both. Maybe you're constantly hearing a subtle hum of "loyalty to the cause," or perhaps you've noticed that certain topics have become, well, sensitive. It can be maddening. But there's good news: you can still hold onto your integrity, keep your head down, and get through this with your values intact. It's all about understanding how to play the game without losing yourself in it.

Welcome to the art of strategic survival—no blind allegiance required.

Practical Tips for Maintaining Integrity Within Restrictive Systems

Let's get one thing clear: operating within a system that doesn't align with your values doesn't mean abandoning those values. It just means navigating your environment with purpose. When public allegiance is prized over private belief, adaptability is key. Here's how to keep your integrity without attracting attention.

Know Your Boundaries and Stick to Them

One of the easiest ways to compromise is by failing to identify where your limits actually lie. Knowing your non-negotiables—those values or actions you won't compromise on—is essential in a restrictive environment. This isn't about waving your beliefs like a flag; it's about knowing where you draw the line so that when a situation tests you, you don't get caught off-guard.

Practical Tip: Write down your core principles and values. Identify what you're willing to "play along" with and where you will hold firm, even if it means some friction. This doesn't need to be a public declaration—keep it as a personal guideline that grounds you.

Stay Neutral in Public Spaces

When in doubt, practice the fine art of neutrality. In meetings, gatherings, or casual conversations, remain mindful of how your words and reactions can be interpreted. Stay calm and nod along without committing yourself to views that contradict your principles. Politicians call it "staying on message." You're just applying it to your daily interactions.

Practical Tip: Keep your responses vague if needed. Instead of agreeing or disagreeing, respond with statements like, "Interesting perspective," or, "I see why some people feel that way." This keeps you out of heated discussions and protects your neutrality. It is generally unwise to go with "Are you freaking kidding me?!?"

Be Consistent, but Selectively Vocal

Consistency is a subtle, powerful tool in restrictive settings. If you're quietly steadfast about certain values (like honesty, respect, or fairness) and demonstrate them consistently, people notice. When you do choose to speak up on issues, your reputation as a reasonable and principled person will serve you well.

Practical Tip: Don't make every small policy change or directive your hill to die on. Choose issues carefully, and when you do voice your opinion, focus on values everyone respects rather than specific political stances. Consistent values-based responses often make a stronger impact than reactions based on temporary frustrations.

How to Interact with Authority Figures and Regulators Without Sacrificing Values

In this environment, dealing with authority figures and regulators isn't just another part of your day—it's an art form. These interactions have the potential to advance your standing or complicate your life, so tread carefully. Here's how to engage with the power players without losing yourself in the process.

Practice Respect without Submission

There's a fine line between showing respect and being deferential. Show respect, but remember that respect doesn't mean submission. Hold your ground politely. In restrictive settings, people often mistake outward politeness for compliance. Being polite is strategic; it keeps the interaction calm and controlled.

Practical Tip: Use non-verbal cues (nods, eye contact) to show you're listening without necessarily agreeing. Use phrases like, "Thank you for sharing your perspective," which shows respect without signaling agreement.

Reframe Expectations as Questions

If someone with authority presents you with directives or requests that feel intrusive, asking clarifying questions can subtly challenge their assumptions. For instance, if there's pressure to engage in activities that feel politically charged, you can respond with questions like, "Could you clarify the objectives for this?" or, "How does this support our goals as a team?"

Practical Tip: Approach directives with a curious mindset rather than outright refusal. Questions that help clarify objectives can sometimes make authority figures rethink the extent of their own expectations, all while positioning you as cooperative.

Use the Power of "Yes, and…" Responses

The classic "Yes, and…" approach (borrowed from improv comedy) can be a powerful tool in challenging environments. Instead of pushing back directly, affirm what's being asked while gently guiding the direction elsewhere. It's a clever way of subtly pivoting without seeming oppositional.

Example: If you're asked to participate in a politically charged event, respond with, "Yes, and I can help by managing the logistical side to keep it running smoothly." You agree to support, but in a way that doesn't require you to take center stage in something you don't align with.

Managing Loyalty Expectations: Responding to Political Pressures Tactfully

When autocratic environments create loyalty tests, the pressure to conform becomes tangible. Whether it's a team-building exercise thinly veiled as a loyalty oath or a friendly reminder about "shared values," these scenarios can be tricky. Here's how to pass the loyalty litmus test without bending your values.

The Art of Passive Participation

In many cases, going through the motions is all that's required. If you're asked to attend an event that feels politically charged, your mere presence is often enough to check the box. Don't feel the need to give 110% if it conflicts with your beliefs— sometimes a simple, low-key presence can keep you under the radar without compromising your principles.

Practical Tip: For events that make you uncomfortable, show up on time, stay quietly involved, and leave promptly when appropriate. This sends the message that you're cooperative without making you a standout advocate. And don't drink the Kool-Aid. Complimentary wine is ok, but if they serve anything bright red, take a hard pass.

Know When to Deploy Strategic Silence

Strategic silence can be your greatest ally. If you're pressed for a statement of loyalty or participation that feels wrong, simply choosing not to answer is sometimes the best option. There's strength in silence, and it can be more disarming than you might think.

Example: If directly asked your opinion on a polarizing topic, consider responding with a diplomatic, "I don't think I know enough to comment." This signals caution without taking sides. It also will likely raise your stature in the other person's esteem as admitting a lack of knowledge on a topic is rare for many people and it conveys a sense of honesty and openness that can be disarming.

Deflect and Refocus

If someone is pressing you to participate in something politically charged, deflect by shifting focus onto a neutral topic or area where you can genuinely contribute. This redirection can steer the conversation away from contentious areas and showcase your commitment to the job without compromising your beliefs.

Practical Tip: If loyalty comes up in a team discussion, redirect focus to a shared project goal or team objective. For instance, "My focus is making sure we hit our targets on [project or goal]." This response subtly communicates that you're committed to the work, not the rhetoric.

The Art of "Staying Under the Radar" While Thriving

Surviving under an autocratic shift often means staying out of the spotlight while still building a life that aligns with your principles. The goal is to find ways to excel without attracting undue attention— achieving personal success without stirring waves.

Excel in Your Domain, Quietly

In restrictive environments, excellence speaks for itself. Your contributions and results don't need a loud spotlight; they simply need to be steady, reliable, and consistent. Aim to excel in your area of expertise, whatever it may be, while keeping the focus on your work rather than drawing attention to yourself.

Practical Tip: When praised, keep responses low-key. A simple "Thank you, I'm glad I could contribute" can deflect excessive attention while reinforcing your role as a team player. Even a simple smile and head nod can be enough to acknowledge the praise but helps create an air of humility that can serve you well in the future.

Build Quiet Alliances

Having allies is crucial in any workplace, but in restrictive environments, subtle support networks are invaluable. Build relationships carefully with people who share your values or, at the very least, respect your approach. These alliances can offer a sense of camaraderie, especially when open expression feels risky.

Practical Tip: Look for coworkers or acquaintances who show small signs of shared values—whether through a book they read, a casual comment, or their general demeanor. Forge connections quietly, offering mutual support without making waves.

Keep Your Personal Views Personal

Keeping a "work version" of yourself separate from the "personal you" is one of the most effective ways to stay under the radar. While this may feel odd or compartmentalized, it's a way to maintain integrity and privacy in an environment where expressing dissent can be risky. Practice keeping your opinions in check without betraying your values.

Practical Tip: Use work-specific social media channels, if needed, or limit personal social media access. Control what you share publicly, and be mindful of who's listening. Maintaining a boundary between your work life and personal beliefs allows you to keep your views private while still showing up authentically in environments that matter to you. In an autocratic system, social media is a tool used by the authorities for whatever purpose they choose. That isn't a paranoid conspiracy thing; it's just fact. Social media is a wonderful tool for police and intelligence services to understand sentiment and standings of groups and individuals. If you can get away with cutting out social media, do it. It will be safer for you and can likely improve your mental wellbeing, too.

Scenario Planning for Business and Career: Navigating an Uncertain Future

In an environment where regulations, market preferences, and political winds can change overnight, planning for "what ifs" becomes essential. Here's how to future-proof your career or business by anticipating shifts and staying adaptable.

Prepare Multiple Income Streams

Economic stability is never guaranteed, and diversification is your best defense. Whether you're an employee or a business owner, consider building alternative income sources that aren't directly tied to a specific sector. This can provide a cushion if political shifts restrict your industry.

Practical Tip: Start freelancing, consulting, or developing an online business that aligns with your skills. Over time, this side income can become a reliable fallback if your primary role becomes unstable.

Invest in Adaptable Skills

Adaptability is your greatest asset. Skills like project management, critical thinking, and digital literacy are valuable across industries. These skills not only increase your employability but also allow you to pivot quickly if policies change or if your job is impacted by regulatory shifts.

Practical Tip: Use online platforms to upskill, focusing on abilities that apply broadly rather than narrowly. This can also help you stay connected to new trends that may arise in different fields, making you a versatile asset.

Network with Resilience in Mind

Networking has always been important, but in restrictive environments, building a resilient, supportive network can be transformative. Focus on connecting with people in varied sectors and keep those relationships active. This diversity gives you access to different perspectives and potential new pathways if things change dramatically.

Practical Tip: When networking, look for people who value resilience and adaptability. Stay in touch by checking in regularly or sharing resources— connections built on mutual support are more likely to last through upheaval. And remember the relationship is a two-way street. Ensure you are providing value and support to your network along the way so making the ask for support when you need it is easier and has a higher likelihood of success.

Holding Onto Your Values: The Long Game

Navigating a shifting political landscape without compromising your beliefs can feel like walking a balance beam during an earthquake, but it's far from impossible. By setting clear boundaries, engaging selectively, and preparing for change, you can protect your values while remaining adaptable to new realities.

Remember, maintaining integrity doesn't have to mean making grand gestures. Sometimes, it's the quiet strength of standing by your principles without fanfare that makes the most impact. Embrace the power of subtlety, choose your battles wisely, and invest in the tools that will carry you through whatever may come.

In the next chapter, we'll dive into the complex world of bureaucracy—not as a roadblock, but as a tool you can leverage to your advantage. You'll discover how to navigate red tape and slow-moving policies to create safety nets, protect yourself, and even use legal channels to secure a measure of control within restrictive systems. We'll also look at examples from history, showing how others have used bureaucracy as a shield in difficult times, proving that even the smallest loopholes can sometimes offer powerful protections.

Chapter 3
Leveraging Bureaucracy to Your Advantage

So, here we are: in a world where bureaucracy—historically the bane of everyone's existence—is about to become your new best friend. I know, I know. Who would have thought that paperwork, red tape, and endless forms would offer anything remotely beneficial? But in a system that values order and compliance above all, learning to navigate the labyrinth can give you an edge.

Consider bureaucracy as the hidden foundation of any stronghold. It's a framework designed to function predictably, to enforce rules, and to slow things down. When wielded strategically, it can be a quiet shield, a way to buy time, or even a method of keeping prying eyes off you. This chapter will help you understand how to use red tape to your advantage, create safety nets, and—because we all need inspiration—highlight a few historical examples where bureaucracy itself became a tool of quiet resistance.

Embracing the Power of Red Tape

If there's one upside to bureaucracy, it's that it's almost annoyingly consistent. Bureaucracies thrive on predictable processes, structured guidelines, and, above all, time. And when things move at a snail's pace, it creates a golden opportunity to use this slowness to your advantage.

Understanding the Loopholes and Delays

Bureaucratic systems are a lot like mazes, complete with dead ends and confusing paths. But this isn't just an annoyance—it's an opportunity. The same red tape that frustrates everyone else can protect you by creating barriers of time and paperwork. Remember, in restrictive systems, decisions that favor you are rarely rushed. By understanding where the delays are, you can use them as a buffer.

Practical Tip: Identify which processes in your organization or community have built-in delays or multiple levels of approval. If you're facing an initiative or directive that puts you at risk, filing for an extension, requesting clarifications, or simply filling out required paperwork carefully (and slowly) can provide a bit of breathing room. Often, requesting "additional information" will buy you time—whether it's a few weeks, a month, or more. Patience here is key; don't underestimate the subtle power of asking questions and dragging out responses.

Keeping Things Technical and Dry

When in doubt, embrace the language of bureaucracy. Instead of objecting outright to new policies, stick to the technical details. Express "concerns" about specific clauses, compliance questions, or logistics, rather than the ideology behind the directive. This slows things down without flashing any red flags.

> Example: Imagine there's a new, highly politicized form of mandatory community engagement. Instead of arguing against its ethics, frame your questions around logistics: "How will we report our involvement? Who will collect the data, and how will it be stored?" Bureaucratic figures love these questions because they involve more rules, more structure. You've just created layers of discussion—layers that give you cover.

Use Bureaucratic Channels as a Stalling Tactic

Filling out forms, submitting requests, and filing appeals are all time-honored ways to pause undesirable action. If you're required to participate in activities or make statements you're uncomfortable with, use the system to create distance. There's no rush to respond to every directive or fill out every form immediately. Remember, filing paperwork is a process, and in a bureaucratic world, every process buys time.

Practical Tip: In an oppressive environment,

don't submit everything on time. Filing on the last day, asking for extensions, or requesting reviews keeps things moving slowly and can even divert attention from you. After all, bureaucracies are designed to process forms and complaints; you're simply exercising your right to take your time.

Thriving in a Deregulated System: What If Bureaucracy Gives Way to Chaos?

So, what happens when the system swings hard in the other direction—when instead of bogging everything down in bureaucracy, the system slashes regulations and fast-tracks decisions? Imagine a scenario where so-called "efficiency" is the new mantra, and leaders are tearing down old structures at record speed to allow "innovation" to reign. With chaos instead of red tape, the game changes, but there are still ways to create order and take advantage of the gaps. Here's how to navigate—and even thrive—in an environment where the rules are constantly in flux.

Stay Agile and Embrace Short-Term Wins

In a chaotic, fast-paced system, flexibility becomes more important than meticulous planning. Regulations may change overnight, and rules you relied on last week could be irrelevant today. Instead of aiming for long-term stability, focus on achieving short-term goals that allow you to adapt as conditions shift. Think of this as "micro-planning" for each phase of chaos, allowing you to benefit from sudden opportunities without committing too much to any one path.

Practical Tip: Start with projects or initiatives that don't require extensive approval or long-term guarantees. For instance, if you're investing, lean toward assets that can adapt quickly to market changes. If you're working on a new business initiative, make it flexible so that it can be modified or redirected if needed.

Exploit the Loopholes in Simplified Regulations

In a rush to streamline operations, chaotic systems often introduce new loopholes as old rules are discarded. Look closely at deregulated policies, which may have broad language or oversights. These "gaps" provide room for creative interpretation and opportunities for action without interference.

Example: If a new "efficiency" policy reduces the number of approvals required for a project, it might also mean there are fewer oversight measures in place. Use this freedom to complete tasks more quickly or push initiatives that align with your goals. Be mindful, though—quick actions under the radar are less likely to attract attention, but they can be questioned if your actions conflict with any remaining policies.

Use the Lack of Oversight to Your Advantage

In a deregulated system, enforcement often takes a backseat to speed. If authorities are too busy pushing through new changes to notice or address everything, you can act more freely. Use this temporary "blind spot" to gain momentum on initiatives or create safeguards for yourself while the system is too preoccupied to scrutinize every move.

Practical Tip: This is the perfect time to establish financial and professional safety nets. Start by securing assets that aren't tied to any regulations in flux, like creating an emergency fund or diversifying income sources. Use this period of leniency to set up structures that will benefit you down the road, whether the chaos continues or order is eventually restored.

Find Allies in the Void of Accountability

In a chaotic environment, having a strong network becomes essential. With fewer regulations to rely on, build alliances with those who can offer support, information, or access to resources. An informal but solid network can help you stay informed, understand where the current power lies, and anticipate where the next shift may come.

Example: Connect with others facing similar uncertainties and form a "support network." If, for example, local inspectors are now skipping certain formalities, those in your network may notice patterns or changes you haven't yet encountered. Sharing these insights allows you to stay agile and make informed decisions as regulations ebb and flow.

Prepare for an Eventual Reset

Deregulated chaos rarely lasts forever. At some point, people begin to demand order, stability, or accountability, especially if chaos leads to major public backlash or failures. Be ready for this swing back toward structure by planning a "reset strategy." Keep track of the regulatory shifts and know which parts of your work or projects could come under scrutiny if order is re-established.

Practical Tip: Don't take extreme risks just because oversight is light. Operate with a moderate level of compliance in areas that may soon regain attention, like taxes, labor laws, or safety regulations. This way, you're prepared to transition smoothly when more structured oversight inevitably returns.

Creating Safety Nets Through Legal and Bureaucratic Channels

If you know the rules, you can find creative ways to protect yourself within them. Bureaucracies are full of rules, loopholes, and exceptions that, when properly used, can give you surprising security. Building these legal and bureaucratic safety nets is less about opposing authority outright and more about creating layers of protection within the structure itself.

Understanding Legal Loopholes and Exceptions

Just like tax codes, bureaucratic systems have exceptions. Some are buried in the fine print, but they're there. Many policies have built-in waivers, hardship clauses, or exemptions for special circumstances. Think of these as built-in "Get Out of Jail Free" cards that might be available if you're savvy enough to ask.

Practical Tip: Research waivers, exemptions, or hardship clauses for any policy you're uncomfortable with. For instance, if there's a mandatory pledge or activity, look into whether you can request a "special consideration" due to personal reasons or logistical challenges. Most systems have these options, though they're not always advertised. Remember, policies can be rigid on the surface but flexible when you know where to apply pressure.

Documentation as a Form of Protection

When living under restrictive systems, documentation becomes your personal insurance policy. Keep detailed records of any interactions, directives, or requests that seem suspect. Bureaucracies run on documentation, so by keeping meticulous records, you create a paper trail that's hard to refute.

Example: If a supervisor or authority figure makes a request that feels borderline inappropriate or political, respond via email, summarizing the interaction and asking for confirmation. This forces the other party to clarify and, in some cases, rethink their approach. Over time, these records serve as both a deterrent and a shield.

Leveraging the Right to Appeal or Review

Many bureaucratic systems allow for a review or appeals process, which can be a lifesaver in an autocratic environment. An appeal buys time, provides a chance to present your side of things, and, in some cases, shifts the attention elsewhere. If you disagree with a decision or directive, filing for a review is a legitimate way to challenge it without outright defiance.

Practical Tip: Even if you don't expect the outcome to change, filing an appeal or requesting a review is often worth it simply for the delay it causes. For added safety, ask for an advocate or advisor to be present in meetings. This introduces additional layers of formality and ensures you're not facing pressure alone.

———————————— ◆ ————————————

Historical Examples of Bureaucracy as a Tool for Shielding and Survival

History has seen its fair share of individuals and communities using bureaucratic tactics to navigate and survive restrictive regimes. These stories remind us that bureaucracies, when used wisely, can serve as a form of subtle resistance, a way to protect oneself without direct confrontation.

1. The Danish Resistance and Paperwork Delay Tactics During World War II, the Danish resistance relied heavily on bureaucratic tactics to delay Nazi demands. Danish

bureaucrats would "lose" Nazi paperwork, insist on unnecessary documentation, or file reports in duplicate—anything to slow down the machine. By creating administrative bottlenecks, they were able to delay deportations and buy time for people to escape.

Lesson: Slowing down the process, whether through "misplaced" forms or procedural delays, can be an effective tool. Even today, small actions—like requiring confirmation on paperwork or introducing extra steps in a process—can keep bureaucratic forces at bay.

2. Soviet Dissidents and Strategic Compliance
   Soviet citizens who disagreed with state policies learned to "comply" in the most technical sense, often performing tasks inefficiently or filing excess reports to distract from actual activities. By working within the system, they used its own sluggishness to shield themselves. They learned to appear compliant on the surface while maintaining a semblance of autonomy beneath the bureaucratic veneer.

Lesson: Bureaucracies can rarely keep up with people who meet every requirement with excessive thoroughness. Even simple actions like over-reporting or creating detailed (but ultimately unhelpful) summaries can create layers of insulation around your true objectives.

3. South African Anti-Apartheid Movement and Bureaucratic Shielding During apartheid, activists used loopholes within South African bureaucracy to operate within the boundaries of the law while still resisting oppression. One tactic was to file for permits for protest gatherings under benign titles to avoid scrutiny. Additionally, activists took advantage of ambiguous administrative processes to evade restrictive laws whenever possible.

Lesson: Bureaucracies often rely on narrow definitions and black-and-white categories. Learning to exploit the gaps between these categories, like applying for permits under neutral terms, can provide a way to operate with minimal oversight.

———————————————— ◆ ————————————————

Final Thoughts on Using Bureaucracy to Your Advantage

Bureaucracy may be a frustrating concept, but it's a powerful one. When wielded with patience, creativity, and just the right amount of subtle defiance, it can serve as a tool for creating breathing room, shielding yourself, and even delaying policies you find difficult to support. Rather than viewing red tape as an obstacle, consider it a game that can be played—strategically, patiently, and with a steady eye on your ultimate goals.

In the next chapter, we'll switch gears and focus

on financial strategies: how to safeguard your resources, make smart investments, and ensure that you're financially prepared for both immediate disruptions and the long game. You'll learn how to build financial resilience and protect your assets in a shifting political and economic landscape. After all, in any storm, it's those who have prepared that weather it best.

Chapter 4
Fortifying Your Finances in Uncertain Times

The prospect of navigating financial uncertainty under an increasingly autocratic system is daunting. For many, financial stability is a cornerstone of personal security, and in restrictive political landscapes, safeguarding your money and assets becomes paramount. It's not just about having enough to get by—it's about building a resilient financial structure that can withstand political turbulence, rapid policy shifts, and economic shocks.

So, let's dive into the world of financial resilience. This chapter will cover strategies for protecting your assets, diversifying income streams, and investing with a safety-first mindset. We'll also look at some unconventional tactics that could make all the difference in a chaotic system. Buckle up—it's time to shore up those defenses.

Understanding and Anticipating Financial Risks

Before diving into specific strategies, let's start with a quick overview of the risks you're facing. Autocratic regimes, especially those prone to erratic policy changes, create a unique set of financial vulnerabilities for individuals and businesses:

- **Regulatory Surprises:** Financial regulations can change overnight, often with little warning or public input.

- **Currency Fluctuations:** Authoritarian economies may experience high inflation, currency devaluation, or fluctuating exchange rates.

- **Increased Taxes and Tariffs:** To fund pet projects or control the economy, autocratic governments often increase taxes or impose tariffs, which can hit your finances hard.

- **Asset Seizure or Frozen Accounts:** In extreme cases, autocratic regimes might seize private assets, limit cash withdrawals, or monitor and freeze accounts.

- **Restricted Investment Options:** Investment choices may narrow as industries or sectors fall out of political favor, making it harder to achieve financial growth.

Let's go into detail on practical steps you can take to protect and grow your finances in an unstable landscape.

Diversify Your Income Streams

One of the most effective ways to build financial resilience is by having multiple income streams. Relying solely on one job or business can make you vulnerable if that sector faces government restrictions or policy changes. Diversifying doesn't mean overextending yourself—it means creating a balance between different sources so that if one falters, you have a backup.

Side Gigs and Freelance Work

Consider taking on freelance work or a side hustle that leverages your existing skills but isn't directly tied to your main job or sector. Freelance platforms, consulting gigs, or online tutoring are all options that can generate income independently of your main job. Plus, freelance work allows for flexibility, which can be crucial if your primary job is affected by political upheaval.

Online Businesses

If you have an entrepreneurial streak, starting an online business can be a great way to create passive income streams. Whether it's an e-commerce store, selling digital products, or launching an educational platform, online businesses can provide flexibility and independence. However, it's essential to keep these ventures low-profile and limit personal information tied to them.

Investments in Real Assets

When cash feels insecure, real assets like real

estate or precious metals can serve as tangible sources of stability. Unlike digital assets or stocks, real assets are harder for governments to restrict or devalue. Although real estate comes with its own set of risks, it can be a strong anchor in uncertain economic times.

Protecting Your Savings and Accounts

In times of political instability, even basic savings accounts can become a point of vulnerability. Here are some tactics to help safeguard your cash and minimize risk:

Diversify Across Financial Institutions

Instead of keeping all your funds in one bank, consider spreading your money across several institutions. This way, if one bank falls out of favor or faces issues due to political interference, you still have access to funds elsewhere. Aim for a mix of large, established banks and smaller credit unions, as each may react differently to political changes.

Maintain a Cash Reserve

In volatile political climates, there's always a risk of restricted bank access or ATM withdrawals. Keep a portion of your emergency fund as physical cash in a safe, accessible location. Don't hoard excessive amounts (as it could invite scrutiny), but have enough for a few weeks' worth of expenses in case of disruptions.

Consider Foreign Currency Accounts

If your country's currency is at risk of devaluation or inflation, consider holding part of your savings in a foreign currency, such as the dollar, euro, or yen. Many banks offer multi-currency accounts, allowing you to hold a mix of currencies. This can act as a hedge if your national currency loses value rapidly.

Limit Digital Footprints in Banking

Autocratic regimes may monitor accounts or transactions to assess an individual's loyalty or detect dissent. Limiting your digital banking activity and conducting more transactions in cash or through alternative channels can help protect your financial privacy. Avoid saving statements or personal information on cloud services or any devices connected to public Wi-Fi.

Building a Resilient Investment Portfolio

Investing during political uncertainty requires a balance between growth and security. In autocratic or volatile settings, traditional investment vehicles may not offer the same security they once did. Here's how to adjust your investment strategy to weather potential instability:

Focus on Low-Risk, Defensive Stocks

Defensive stocks—those in essential industries like healthcare, utilities, or consumer goods—tend to perform well even in economic downturns. These sectors are less likely to be targeted by shifting policies and can provide consistent returns even when the broader market struggles. Consider allocating a portion of your portfolio to defensive stocks to reduce risk.

Explore Tangible Assets

When stock markets become unpredictable, tangible assets—like real estate, commodities (such as gold and silver), or even farmland—can offer a layer of security. Real assets retain intrinsic value, are less likely to be impacted by currency fluctuations, and provide more stability in uncertain times.

International Investment Funds

If domestic investments feel too risky, international funds can offer diversification and reduce exposure to national policy shifts. Look for mutual funds or exchange-traded funds (ETFs) with holdings spread across politically stable countries. This strategy allows you to benefit from growth in more stable economies without direct exposure to national policies.

Cryptocurrencies with Caution

Cryptocurrencies offer potential independence from traditional financial systems, but they are not without risk. Autocratic governments may impose regulations, restrict access, or monitor cryptocurrency transactions. If you choose to invest in cryptocurrencies, do so cautiously, keep your holdings secure, and stay updated on regulatory changes.

Financial Opportunism in Uncertain Systems: Risk or Reward?

In autocratic or politically unstable systems, financial opportunities often arise in unique and sometimes ethically ambiguous ways. Industries tied to state priorities, like security, infrastructure, and resource extraction, may offer rapid growth, subsidies, or other benefits. The choice to engage in these ventures can be lucrative, but it comes with its own set of considerations.

So, is it worth it? Let's examine the practical and ethical dimensions of capitalizing on financial opportunities within restrictive systems.

Practical Opportunities in Politically Favored Sectors

As governments consolidate control, certain industries often become strategic priorities. These can include defense, technology, energy, construction, and media. Businesses within these sectors may receive substantial government support, subsidies, or preferential regulations. For investors and entrepreneurs, this can translate into high growth potential with a degree of financial insulation from market volatility.

Examples of Practical Gains:

- Government Contracts: Many autocratic regimes push state-funded projects, such as infrastructure development or tech initiatives. Partnering with the government can open doors to lucrative contracts, steady income streams, and market monopolies.

- Limited Competition: When governments favor certain companies or industries, competition may diminish, either through regulation or intimidation of competitors. This can create a protected market for those aligned with state interests.

- Access to Resources: In some cases, the state might grant favored businesses or industries easier access to resources like land, utilities, or materials, reducing overhead and bolstering profit margins.

Ethical Considerations: Values vs. Financial Gains

While financial rewards may be appealing, aligning too closely with an authoritarian system often involves a degree of compromise. Ethical considerations come into play, especially if the industry in question is linked to practices that may conflict with personal values, such as surveillance, censorship, or monopolistic control.

Balancing Personal Integrity:

- Evaluate the Nature of the Work: Assess whether the work directly contributes to or enables actions you find objectionable. For instance, developing infrastructure may feel neutral, while contributing to surveillance technology may cross a personal line.

- Set Boundaries on Engagement: Consider ways to engage without fully committing your brand or reputation to state initiatives. For example, working on smaller contracts or subcontracting rather than taking a lead role allows for a degree of separation.

- Consider Long-Term Consequences: Partnering too closely with an authoritarian government can create reputational risks, especially if political tides change. Weigh potential short-term gains against the impact on your future career or brand.

Practical Tips for Ethical Financial Opportunism

For those who decide to explore these opportunities, there are ways to minimize ethical conflicts while remaining financially strategic. Consider these tips to engage with state-favored opportunities on your own terms:

- Stay Informed on Policy Shifts: Political priorities can change quickly in authoritarian regimes. Stay up-to-date on government announcements, as shifts in policy can both create and remove financial opportunities.

- Limit Exposure to Controversial Sectors: If possible, prioritize work in neutral or low-risk areas—such as infrastructure or utilities—rather than high-risk sectors like defense or surveillance. You can benefit from financial stability without direct involvement in controversial state initiatives.

- Collaborate with Ethical Partners: Work with organizations that emphasize ethical practices, even if they operate within favored sectors. Partnerships can provide a buffer and help you navigate the system more comfortably.

- Keep an Eye Towards Legacy: Remember that the current political or governmental climate might change (if history is any judge, most modern autocracies springing up in regions with a history of democracy, do not last long) and your actions will be viewed through the lens of the victor. No judgement here on what you decide to do but it's generally a good idea to not be evil.

Hypothetical Scenario: Navigating State-Favored Projects with Personal Integrity

Imagine you're a contractor with expertise in infrastructure development. The government has just announced a massive state-funded initiative to improve public infrastructure, and there's significant financial incentive to participate. However, some elements of the project are linked to government control over public spaces, and you feel uneasy about certain aspects of how the spaces may be used for surveillance or political events.

In this scenario, here's how you could balance financial opportunity with ethical considerations:

1. Set Boundaries on Scope: Instead of committing to the full project, consider limiting your involvement to aspects that align with public welfare, like safety improvements or sustainability measures. This way, you contribute positively without being directly involved in elements that conflict with your values.

2. Focus on Neutral Contributions: Frame your work as an enhancement of community welfare and avoid taking on aspects that directly support government control. For example, if asked to include surveillance infrastructure, suggest alternative ways to improve public security that don't infringe on privacy, or simply opt not to participate in that part of the project.

3. Collaborate with Ethical Partners: If possible, team up with subcontractors or partners who share your values and are also committed to ethical practices. Having like-minded collaborators reinforces your stance and keeps you aligned with a shared commitment to integrity.

4. Document Your Contributions: Keep detailed records of your contributions, ensuring transparency. If political tides shift or if you're ever asked to justify your involvement, you can point to the neutral or constructive role you played. This documentation allows you

to take advantage of the financial opportunity while protecting your reputation in case the project's associations become controversial.

By taking these steps, you balance practicality with ethics, making a positive impact within the parameters of the system without feeling compromised.

Financial Privacy and Security

In a restrictive environment, maintaining financial privacy becomes crucial to avoiding unnecessary attention. Here are some strategies for enhancing your financial privacy:

Use Encrypted Communication

Discussing financial plans and investments in an autocratic setting can be risky if conversations are not secure. Use encrypted messaging apps for discussions related to your financial strategies, especially if you're discussing sensitive matters with trusted contacts.

Avoid Social Media Bragging

While sharing financial milestones or investments online is common, it's best to keep these accomplishments private in a restrictive setting. Social media can quickly turn against you, and public displays of wealth may invite scrutiny or even punitive measures in politically tense times.

Practice Digital Hygiene

In politically restrictive environments, your online

presence and digital activities can be subject to scrutiny. Taking steps to protect your financial privacy can be crucial. Here are practical tips that can add an extra layer of security:

1. Use a VPN (Virtual Private Network): A VPN encrypts your internet connection, making it harder for third parties to monitor your online activities. This can protect sensitive browsing related to finances or political conversations. Choose a reputable VPN provider with a no-logs policy and a strong history of user security.

2. Encrypted Email Services: Consider using encrypted email platforms like ProtonMail or Tutanota for financial communications. These services offer end-to-end encryption, which means only you and the recipient can read the emails. This extra layer of privacy is useful for protecting sensitive financial discussions or backup plans.

3. Secure Your Devices with Multi-Factor Authentication (MFA): Enable MFA on any accounts containing sensitive financial or personal information. This extra layer of security ensures that, even if your password is compromised, unauthorized access to your accounts is more difficult.

4. Limit Use of Cloud-Based Storage for Financial Documents: Avoid storing sensitive financial documents or backup plans in cloud

services, especially those accessible across devices. If you need digital copies, consider using a secure, encrypted USB drive that's kept offline or a password-protected local folder on your personal device.

5. Avoid Public Wi-Fi for Financial Transactions: Public Wi-Fi networks are vulnerable to hacking, making it easy for malicious actors to intercept your data. Use your cellular data or a secure, private Wi-Fi connection when conducting any financial transactions or accessing sensitive accounts.

By incorporating these digital hygiene habits, you protect your financial activities from potential monitoring or interference, allowing you greater control over your privacy in an uncertain environment.

Debt Management and Cash Flow Optimization

Debt can be a double-edged sword in uncertain times. Here's how to approach debt and cash flow management to ensure stability:

Prioritize Paying Off High-Interest Debt

In volatile climates, the last thing you need is the added burden of high-interest debt. Focus on paying down any existing high-interest loans or credit card debt. Not only does this improve your cash flow, but it also reduces dependency on financial institutions.

Build a Flexible Budget

Traditional budgets may not work well in unpredictable times. Instead, focus on flexible budgeting by allocating a portion of your income toward essentials, a portion for savings, and a portion for discretionary expenses. Having a flexible budget helps you adjust quickly if expenses or income sources change suddenly.

Delay Major Purchases

Unless necessary, avoid significant purchases that tie up large portions of your cash reserves. Major purchases can drain your liquidity, leaving you vulnerable if financial conditions shift. Instead, prioritize smaller purchases that enhance your quality of life without draining resources.

Establishing a Network of Financial Allies

Financial resilience in uncertain times is not just about securing your own resources—it's about creating a network of trusted allies who can offer advice, support, or even funding if needed. Here's how to build a network that contributes to your financial security:

Identify Trusted Professionals

Seek out reliable financial advisors, accountants, and lawyers who are skilled at navigating restrictive environments. Having professionals who understand the local landscape can provide valuable insights and help you stay compliant with shifting regulations.

Develop a Peer Support Group

Create or join a peer support group with individuals who share your goals and values. Together, you can exchange financial tips, share resources, and even collaborate on projects that offer mutual benefit. This network can provide moral and practical support during challenging times.

Tap Into Alternative Funding Sources

In uncertain financial environments, traditional loans may be harder to obtain, but alternative funding sources—such as community lending circles, investment clubs, or peer-to-peer lending networks—can provide liquidity when needed. Just ensure these arrangements are trustworthy and legally sound.

Closing Thoughts on Financial Fortification

In an unpredictable political landscape, financial security becomes a strategic game, one that requires foresight, flexibility, and resourcefulness. From diversified income streams and resilient investments to digital privacy and a solid network, building financial resilience isn't just a matter of protecting what you have—it's about ensuring you can adapt, grow, and thrive even when the world around you feels shaky.

In the next chapter, we'll delve into the nuances of subtle dissent in business and media, examining how to maintain integrity in restricted environments without attracting undue attention. With the right strategies, you can communicate your values, keep your creative integrity, and foster quiet resilience in your professional life—even when the pressure to conform is at its highest.

Chapter 5
Subtle Dissent in Business & Media

When the air grows thick with restrictive policies, public compliance becomes the norm, and creative or journalistic integrity can start to feel like a risky luxury. Yet history has proven that even under authoritarian rule, individuals have found ways to express dissent, challenge narratives, and engage audiences—all while staying under the radar. Subtle dissent isn't about grand gestures or direct defiance; it's about using strategy, creativity, and timing to communicate meaningfully without setting off alarms.

In this chapter, we'll explore methods to keep your integrity intact in restrictive environments, including tactics for pushing boundaries with finesse and connecting with audiences who share your values.

Maintaining Integrity in Restrictive Environments

Maintaining your core principles while working in a restrictive environment is no small feat. It requires navigating a fine line between expressing truth and staying safe. Here are ways to hold onto your integrity when the stakes are high:

Embed Truth in Ambiguity

Ambiguity can be a powerful tool in environments that suppress overt expressions of dissent. Sometimes, the best way to communicate ideas without drawing attention is to layer meaning into your work so that only those who are looking closely understand the full message.

Example: Think of a journalist covering government policies. Rather than bluntly criticizing policy changes, they might use factual reporting that highlights statistics, contrasting historical examples, or indirect quotes. For instance, covering a new law, they could mention past policies in other countries that failed, allowing the audience to draw their own conclusions.

Use Symbolism and Metaphors

Symbolism and metaphor are age-old methods for expressing ideas without explicit statements. Art, literature, and journalism often contain layers of meaning that can bypass censorship because they're not immediately obvious. Readers who resonate with the message will recognize it, while others may see it as harmless or ambiguous.

> Example: Artists or writers might use recurring symbols, like imagery of walls, broken bridges, or shadows, to subtly critique restrictive governance. In countries where nature imagery is less controlled, journalists might frame reports using metaphors related to natural cycles, like "seasons changing," to suggest political shifts without explicitly stating opposition.

Choose Your Medium Carefully

Certain formats offer more creative flexibility. For instance, podcasts, opinion pieces, and satire tend to allow more leeway for commentary, often due to their indirect nature. When creating under restrictions, picking a format that naturally lends itself to subtlety can be advantageous.

> Example: In radio or podcast formats, a host might share seemingly innocent anecdotes or "parables" that encourage listeners to think critically about broader issues. For instance, discussing the story of someone who navigated bureaucracy creatively can inspire resilience without mentioning any specific government entity.

Strategies for Subtly Pushing Boundaries Without Direct Confrontation

When censorship tightens, pushing boundaries requires a deft hand and a creative mind. Here are strategies for making your message resonate without setting off alarms:

Lean on Data, Facts, and Context

Facts can speak for themselves, especially when placed in context. Data-based arguments often allow you to convey ideas that would seem confrontational if phrased directly. Presenting neutral data without commentary invites the audience to form their own interpretations, which can be surprisingly powerful.

Example: Imagine a report on employment rates that casually compares rates in certain sectors over time or between regions. You don't need to say, "These policies hurt employment"— simply show that jobs in specific industries have decreased sharply since a certain law was enacted.

Use Humor and Satire (Cautiously)

Humor and satire can be effective for criticism, as they allow you to comment on serious issues with a layer of ambiguity. Satire in particular can highlight contradictions and absurdities without making direct accusations. However, it's essential to gauge how humor will be received and whether it could be easily misinterpreted or deemed offensive by authorities.

Example: A cartoonist might create a series of images poking fun at daily inconveniences caused by policy changes. These images seem innocuous but become a lighthearted critique recognized by the audience. Or, in a journalistic piece, you might include a playful comment about "the joys of endless paperwork" when discussing a new regulation, signaling to readers that they're not alone in their frustration.

Rely on Familiar Tropes and Archetypes

Using well-known archetypes allows you to communicate nuanced ideas indirectly. Characters that readers instantly recognize can represent societal roles or challenges without naming names. Familiar tropes also resonate with people on a deeper level, tapping into shared stories that have existed for generations.

Example: In a business environment, writers or media producers can frame stories about "visionary leaders" or "misguided innovators," hinting at real-world figures or policies through allegorical storytelling. This way, you address current issues under the guise of discussing universally relatable archetypes.

Amplify Voices from the Ground

When official narratives dominate, amplifying grassroots voices can be a powerful form of subtle dissent. Sharing testimonials, insights, or stories from individuals affected by policies or decisions can challenge dominant narratives without requiring explicit critique. Through their stories, you allow readers to see the human impact of abstract policies.

> Example: Journalists might focus on interviewing small business owners, students, or healthcare workers. A collection of these firsthand perspectives offers an authentic critique of the status quo without requiring commentary from the writer. Readers can empathize with the individuals, creating a powerful form of silent dissent.

Communicating Indirectly with an Audience that Shares Your Values

Building rapport with an audience that shares your values in a restrictive environment requires trust and subtlety. Here are techniques for communicating without explicitly stating your views:

Use Subtle Signals

In situations where outright expressions could be risky, subtle signals can help identify and connect with like-minded individuals. Shared language, references to certain books, or even recurring phrases can signal mutual understanding. It's akin to a coded language that those "in the know" will recognize.

> Example: A blogger might close each article with a quote from a classic work known for its themes of freedom and resilience. Over time, readers who value these principles come to recognize the sign-off as a discreet affirmation of shared values.

Create Spaces for Dialogue

When direct discourse is risky, creating controlled spaces for discussion can provide a safe platform for exchanging ideas. Private networks, invitation-only newsletters, and encrypted groups allow for open dialogue without risking broader exposure. These platforms can nurture meaningful exchange and offer a sense of community.

> Example: A journalist might create an email newsletter for select readers or start a private group chat where discussions about sensitive topics can happen safely. The group provides an avenue for connection and dialogue, while the enclosed format adds a layer of protection.

Leverage "Safe" Topics to Make Broader Points

Certain subjects—like art, history, and literature—often provide a safe platform for discussing values and principles without sparking suspicion. By weaving historical or literary references into your work, you can address themes that are relevant to your audience while avoiding direct criticism.

> Example: If you're a business writer, you might cover historical entrepreneurs who faced challenges from their governments, drawing parallels to today's climate. This approach uses historical distance to reflect on current issues subtly, resonating with those who share your concerns without directly addressing the present context.

———————— ✦ ————————

Case Study: Dissident Expression Through Literature in the USSR

One of the most famous examples of subtle dissent in restrictive environments comes from the Soviet Union, where writers and artists used creativity to express dissent without direct confrontation. Author Mikhail Bulgakov, for instance, crafted The Master and Margarita, a novel filled with satire, allegory, and absurdism, which offered scathing critiques of Soviet bureaucracy, censorship, and paranoia without explicitly targeting Soviet leadership.

Key Techniques Used in Bulgakov's Work:

- Symbolism and Allegory: By creating a supernatural narrative filled with hidden symbols, Bulgakov offered a way for readers to interpret themes about state control and moral decay in their own way.

- Humor and Satire: Through his characters and plotlines, Bulgakov used humor to expose the absurdities of Soviet life. Readers recognized the parallels without the author needing to openly criticize the state.

- Ambiguity and Open Interpretation: Bulgakov avoided making his message overt. The book's layered meanings allowed readers to interpret it in ways that resonated with their own experiences of the Soviet system.

Relevance Today: While we may not be writing

novels under Soviet rule, the techniques Bulgakov used are still applicable. Humor, symbolism, and ambiguity remain powerful tools for expressing subtle dissent and connecting with like-minded audiences in restrictive environments. His work is a testament to the fact that storytelling, when done artfully, can challenge narratives even under heavy censorship.

Final Thoughts on Subtle Dissent

In restrictive environments, pushing back doesn't always mean making grand gestures. Often, the most effective forms of dissent are quiet, steady, and clever. By embedding truth in ambiguity, choosing your medium wisely, and communicating through coded language or symbolism, you can maintain your integrity and connect with others who share your values. Whether you're in media, business, or any creative field, remember that you have the power to subtly influence the conversation, invite critical thinking, and encourage resilience.

In the next chapter, we'll shift our focus to building alliances and fostering networks of trust in restrictive environments. We'll explore how to form meaningful connections with others who share your values, create support systems outside of official channels, and build resilient communities. By looking at case studies of businesses and communities that have helped each other survive in authoritarian settings, you'll discover practical ways to forge networks that not only support individual resilience but also strengthen collective integrity. The power of community is invaluable—especially when the world around you feels unpredictable.

Chapter 6
Community Building and Networks of Trust

Navigating life and business under authoritarian rule is challenging, but one of the most powerful tools you can wield is the strength of community. Whether it's finding allies who share your values, creating informal support networks, or working together to protect each other, these alliances offer both resilience and solidarity in restrictive environments. However, it's essential to approach community-building with care, especially when dealing with regimes that may use informants to disrupt connections. In this chapter, we'll explore how to build networks of trust that can withstand scrutiny while supporting both individual and collective well-being.

Let's dive into how you can forge connections with like-minded individuals, create support systems outside of official channels, and learn from historical examples of resilience in communities facing autocratic challenges.

Building Alliances with Those Who Value Freedom and Integrity

In a society where freedom and integrity are increasingly at risk, finding people who share your values can feel like a lifeline. Like-minded individuals not only offer support but also provide insight, resources, and a sense of solidarity. However, in an environment that might encourage distrust or reporting, connecting with the right people is a subtle art that requires awareness and discretion.

Finding Allies Discreetly

Networking in a restrictive setting means choosing allies with care. Look for individuals who demonstrate subtle signs of shared values without needing direct affirmation. Notice small details: the books they read, the conversations they avoid, or the causes they support through quiet gestures. People who value freedom and integrity often reveal these principles through everyday actions.

Practical Tips for Discreet Networking:

- Observe First, Approach Slowly: People in restrictive environments may be cautious, so allow time to get to know their character before initiating deeper conversations. Trust is best built gradually, without appearing eager or probing too quickly.

- Common Interests as a Gateway: Engaging in casual conversations about shared interests—such as community events, safe cultural topics, or professional challenges—can lay the groundwork for more meaningful exchanges later.

- Signal Shared Values Subtly: If you feel safe, small cues such as a thoughtful comment or mentioning a known supporter of freedom and integrity can signal shared values. If the person responds positively, you may have found a potential ally.

Balancing Caution with Connection

While it's essential to build alliances, it's equally important to balance connection with caution. Many authoritarian regimes actively encourage people to report each other, which can strain the development of trust. You can avoid unnecessary exposure by maintaining a low profile and remembering that alliances in such environments work best with mutual respect and measured trust.

Creating Support Systems Outside Official Channels

In an authoritarian setting, it's often wise to build support systems that operate outside of formal or government-approved channels. These informal networks can offer a sense of safety and a source of practical resources, from information to moral support. Establishing these systems means working creatively and flexibly, finding ways to maintain independence without attracting undue attention.

Grassroots Networks for Mutual Aid

Mutual aid networks are a powerful tool for community resilience. In these networks, members pool resources, knowledge, and support to help each other weather difficult times. Whether it's sharing food, medical supplies, or even legal advice, grassroots networks foster resilience by creating a web of support that does not rely on state approval.

Examples of Mutual Aid Networks:

- Healthcare Assistance: Some communities have established informal networks to help those in need of medical care, especially where government restrictions make it difficult to access services without strict compliance.

- Resource Sharing: Shared food pantries, neighborhood barter systems, and emergency funds allow communities to provide for each other in ways that stay off the radar.

- Legal and Educational Support: Some networks offer informal legal advice or educational tutoring outside government programs, helping individuals maintain autonomy and knowledge in an increasingly regulated environment.

Secure Communication Channels for Trusted Connections

For those seeking to organize or share sensitive information, secure communication channels are essential. Messaging apps with end-to-end encryption (like Signal) or offline meetings in trusted spaces can help protect the privacy of participants. Always be mindful of digital hygiene and make it a practice to check security features regularly, as authoritarian governments are known for monitoring online communication.

Best Practices for Secure Communication:

- Use Encrypted Platforms: Choose messaging platforms with strong encryption protocols, ideally with disappearing messages or no saved chat histories.

- Limit Digital Exposure: Avoid sharing personal or sensitive information in public or unsecure online spaces. If discussing sensitive topics, do so in person or through encrypted calls.

- Rotate Meeting Spaces: If you gather in person, change locations to avoid drawing patterns that could be easily tracked.

Learning from History: Case Studies of Resilient Communities

Throughout history, communities under restrictive regimes have found creative ways to support each other while remaining resilient. Here, we look at a few examples that illustrate the power of solidarity and the ingenuity of those who formed networks despite the challenges.

Case Study 1: The Polish Solidarity Movement (1980s)

In the 1980s, Poland's Solidarity movement emerged as a powerful labor union and social movement that stood up to the communist government. While initially focused on workers' rights, Solidarity quickly grew into a broader movement advocating for political reform. Despite government crackdowns, Solidarity continued to organize through underground networks, leveraging a combination of coded communication, trusted alliances, and community support.

Lessons from Solidarity:

- Strength in Numbers: Solidarity's leaders knew that even under pressure, they were less vulnerable together than alone. By coordinating quiet support among workers, academics, and religious figures, the movement maintained strength without centralized control.

- Coded Communication: Solidarity leaders used coded language in print media and public speeches, allowing members to communicate discreetly. Small, subtle symbols or phrases conveyed support without directly challenging authorities.

Case Study 2: The Underground Libraries in Sarajevo (1990s)

During the Bosnian War, Sarajevo was besieged for nearly four years, and the residents were cut off from the outside world. In response, a network of underground libraries emerged, where citizens gathered to share books, teach classes, and exchange ideas. These libraries became a beacon of intellectual freedom and unity, allowing people to retain their identity even in the harshest conditions.

Lessons from Sarajevo:

- Culture as Resistance: By preserving culture and education, Sarajevo's residents found a way to resist without overt defiance. The libraries became a subtle act of protest against the isolation and hardship imposed by the conflict.

- Community Strength in Small Acts: The libraries operated quietly, with no grand proclamations. By focusing on small, community-based acts of resistance, they created a network of resilience that was difficult for authorities to dismantle.

Case Study 3: China's Underground Churches

China's underground churches are another example of communities that have formed networks under restrictive regimes. Operating outside of state-sanctioned religious institutions, underground churches rely on trust-based networks and small gatherings. Members connect discreetly, often using homes or rotating venues for worship, creating a resilient, decentralized structure that adapts to crackdowns and surveillance.

Lessons from Underground Churches:

- Decentralized Structure: By avoiding large gatherings and using informal leadership, underground churches have been able to persist without relying on central organization. This model reduces vulnerability to targeted crackdowns.

- Resilient Networks of Trust: Personal trust is the foundation of these networks, with members forming connections through shared values and quiet allegiance to their beliefs.

Building and maintaining informal networks of support has been a successful strategy for people living under various restrictive regimes. From underground resistance movements in Nazi-occupied Europe to the solidarity networks that operated under the Soviet Union, people have often relied on unofficial alliances to survive, resist, and ultimately rebuild. When official channels fail or turn against the population, these alliances become a critical lifeline. History offers numerous examples of communities that supported one another in times of hardship—and, in some cases, even managed to outlast the very systems that oppressed them.

But historical examples aren't the only ones that

illuminate the value of resilient networks. During my time working counter-insurgency operations in Iraq and Afghanistan, I witnessed firsthand how informal networks of support could make or break the success of resistance movements. While many factors contributed to the outcome of these efforts, the groups that succeeded in resisting occupation often did so because of the strength of their networks. These networks, built on mutual trust and shared goals, operated under the radar yet were highly effective in pooling resources, sharing information, and providing critical support.

Their success didn't come without risks, though—when networks were compromised, they faced severe consequences. But more often than not, their ability to operate discreetly while maintaining strong connections provided them with a resilience that outlasted formal structures. This is why building alliances and networks is so crucial when navigating an authoritarian landscape. By drawing on the lessons learned in these conflict zones, we can see that it's possible to build strong, supportive communities even under restrictive conditions. It's all about finding the right balance between connection and caution.

Whether in conflict zones or autocratic societies, these resilient communities understood that solidarity wasn't just a strategy; it was essential for survival. From sharing resources to distributing news and even providing basic education, people within these networks found ways to resist and support one another under the most challenging circumstances. For those navigating authoritarian shifts today, these historical and contemporary examples remind us that networks, when built carefully, can offer a vital source of strength and support.

———————— ◆ ————————

Building Networks Safely: Balancing Caution and Trust

As critical as these networks are, it's essential to remember that autocratic regimes often encourage people to inform on their neighbors, friends, and even family members. Authoritarian systems thrive on distrust, and the encouragement of reporting dissent creates an atmosphere where trust must be handled carefully. It's possible to build strong networks without compromising safety, but it requires discernment and an understanding of the risks involved.

Just as successful insurgent groups in conflict zones managed to balance connection with caution, so must individuals building networks in restrictive political climates today. Focus on relationships with people who have demonstrated consistent values and a willingness to support each other. Start with small acts of mutual assistance to build trust gradually. As you extend your network, maintain discretion and avoid discussing sensitive matters in public or unsecured settings.

The ability to operate quietly while maintaining strong connections—just as those successful insurgent groups did—underscores the power of resilient, discreet communities. By adopting similar approaches, individuals in today's political landscape can develop networks that provide support, safety, and shared purpose without attracting unnecessary attention.

Understand the Risks of Infiltration

In regimes that rely on informants, infiltration is a common tactic to disrupt communities and create an atmosphere of fear. As you build connections, be mindful of the risk that people may report activities or conversations. Recognizing this doesn't mean abandoning the idea of connection—it simply means choosing your allies carefully.

Strategies for Avoiding Infiltration:

- Limit Sensitive Information Sharing: Keep sensitive information on a need-to-know basis. If you're organizing or sharing important information, avoid discussing details with casual acquaintances.

- Test Trust Gradually: Start by sharing non-sensitive ideas or resources before moving to more significant topics. Trust can be built slowly, with individuals who consistently respect your privacy and demonstrate integrity.

- Stay Aware of Sudden Involvement: Be

cautious of new individuals who seem overly eager to connect or who push for specific information or involvement. True allies will respect a gradual approach to building trust.

Fostering Mutual Support Without Exposure

Building networks of support can be done in ways that limit exposure. Engaging in acts of mutual aid—like sharing resources or knowledge—without delving into personal views or politics allows you to maintain community resilience without drawing attention.

Practical Tips for Mutual Support:

- Focus on Shared Goals: Keep activities focused on mutual benefit, like sharing skills, resources, or educational opportunities. This can offer practical support without the need to reveal individual ideologies.

- Create Layers of Involvement: Not everyone in your network needs to be equally informed or involved. Some allies can be closer confidants, while others might participate in more casual ways, offering help without deep engagement.

- Be Transparent with Trusted Allies: For your most trusted allies, honesty is important. Communicate openly about the need for discretion and the risks associated with the network. People who share your goals will understand the value of caution.

Case Study: How Informal Networks Helped Families in East Germany

Following this historical and personal context, we can draw a parallel with the informal networks that helped families survive in East Germany under the Stasi regime. Neighbors, friends, and co-workers quietly banded together, passing along news and resources and even providing emotional support that was otherwise lacking in such a rigid, surveillance-heavy society. These connections, though discreet, were crucial in allowing people to endure the difficulties of life under constant watch. In a similar way, people today can cultivate supportive networks that offer stability without putting them at risk.

By keeping these case studies in mind, you can begin to understand the importance of quiet but resilient networks. Just as informal support networks have helped people through oppressive periods in the past, these relationships can offer strength and protection today. Practicing caution, learning from history, and fostering strong but careful connections can help you build the kind of support network that not only helps you endure but may, in time, help you thrive.

Closing Thoughts on Building Resilient Networks

In authoritarian environments, community networks serve as both protection and resistance. By carefully building alliances, supporting each other through informal channels, and remaining aware of potential risks, you can foster a network that not only upholds your values but also offers stability amid political turbulence.

By fostering connections with trusted individuals who share your values, creating support systems that operate independently of official channels, and learning from historical examples, you're laying the groundwork for a resilient network. You don't need to go it alone, but you do need to be careful about who you trust.

In the next chapter, we'll turn our focus to personal and family resilience. You'll gain practical techniques for staying mentally strong in politically charged times, learn ways to keep a calm, secure environment at home, and explore strategies for financial and long-term well-being. Together, these steps will help you and your loved ones stay grounded, prepared, and resilient in any circumstance.

Chapter 7
Protecting Personal and Family Resilience

In times of political upheaval, maintaining personal and family resilience is essential. This isn't just about being prepared for physical challenges—it's about fortifying mental and emotional reserves, creating stability for loved ones, and securing financial well-being. Resilience in these times is a skill you can cultivate, one that empowers you to face challenges with confidence, clarity, and peace of mind.

Building resilience isn't just about weathering a single storm; it's about developing the strength to endure multiple waves, adapting as political climates shift around you. Here's how to ensure you and your family remain resilient, grounded, and prepared.

Practical Techniques for Mental Resilience in Politically Charged Times

In an environment where public discourse is polarized and stress is high, mental resilience becomes a lifeline. It's about creating an inner anchor that helps you stay calm, respond thoughtfully, and avoid emotional burnout. Here are key strategies to maintain mental resilience, even as the world around you feels chaotic.

Mindfulness and Centering Practices

Mental resilience starts with awareness of how your thoughts and emotions react to stress. Mindfulness techniques, which focus on being present without judgment, are invaluable. Regular mindfulness exercises—like deep breathing, meditation, or grounding techniques—can help you manage stress effectively. For example, taking five minutes each morning to sit quietly, breathe deeply, and focus on the present moment can recalibrate your stress levels and help you feel more balanced.

Example: During the COVID-19 pandemic, healthcare workers who practiced mindfulness and deep-breathing techniques reported lower levels of stress and burnout, even during peak moments of the crisis. These techniques work by reducing the body's stress response and can be just as effective in politically tense climates.

Establishing Boundaries with Media Consumption

In politically charged times, constant media

exposure can lead to emotional fatigue. Setting boundaries with news and social media—like limiting your screen time, curating your feeds to include positive content, or scheduling breaks from media—can help prevent overload. Instead of scrolling endlessly and counting the ways the world might end, try setting a 'one-news-hour-a-day' rule. Think of it as a diet, but with far fewer calories and a lot less stress. This can provide a balanced view without overwhelming your mental space.

Case Study: Many psychological studies after major events, such as natural disasters and terrorist attacks, have shown that excessive news consumption contributes to anxiety and trauma. Limiting exposure to only what's essential can create a healthier, more resilient mental state.

Building a Daily Routine of Small Wins

When the world around you feels unpredictable, daily routines can create a sense of stability. Focusing on small, manageable tasks—like exercising, cooking, or even organizing your space—provides a sense of accomplishment. These routines become anchors, reminding you that you control certain parts of your life, even in turbulent times.

Tip: Start the day by listing three small, achievable tasks. Completing them, even when larger problems loom, reinforces a sense of capability and normalcy. For families, integrating routines, like shared dinners or weekend activities, can bring calm and familiarity.

Cultivating an Inner Circle of Trust

In challenging times, it's crucial to have a network of people you trust. Creating a small group of family members or friends who understand your values and concerns can provide emotional support, perspective, and encouragement. Regular check-ins, open conversations, and mutual support can bolster everyone's resilience. Take a page from Robert de Niro in Meet the Fockers and invite people into your own circle of trust.

Example: In authoritarian regimes, underground networks of friends and neighbors often provided emotional refuge and essential news. By creating a circle of trusted individuals, you can share insights, advice, and reminders that you're not facing these challenges alone.

Finding Resilience Through Cultural and Spiritual Practices

In times of uncertainty, connecting with familiar cultural or spiritual practices can provide a deep sense of comfort and stability. These traditions, passed down through generations, often carry wisdom on handling adversity and finding inner peace. Embracing these practices as part of your daily routine can strengthen your resilience and bring grounding perspectives in challenging times.

Example: Consider the practice of gratitude, which is woven into many cultural and religious traditions. Setting aside a few moments each day to reflect on what you're grateful for—even small things like a warm meal or a supportive conversation—can foster a positive mindset. Research has shown that regularly practicing gratitude reduces stress and increases overall well-being, helping individuals feel more grounded and less overwhelmed.

Another example is the practice of prayer or meditation. For many people, taking time to connect with a higher power or simply pause for mindful reflection offers a sense of peace and continuity. For instance, in various Indigenous cultures, connecting with nature or performing small, reverent rituals (like lighting incense or singing a prayer) is a way to feel grounded in one's identity and place within the world. Similarly, mindfulness meditation—a practice with roots in Buddhism—can calm the mind, helping individuals build resilience against stress by staying present and avoiding anxious thoughts about the future.

Even if you're not religious, these practices can be adapted in a way that's meaningful to you. Creating a short, daily ritual that's uniquely yours—a gratitude journal, a quiet moment with tea, or a walk in nature—can be a powerful reminder of resilience and stability in the face of life's challenges.

Sometimes, all it takes to feel like you have it together is crossing off 'drink coffee' from your list. If you need to start small, trust me—this counts.

Preparing Family Members for Shifts and Maintaining a Calm Environment at Home

It's natural for family members, particularly children, to pick up on tensions. Maintaining a steady, calm home environment becomes vital in helping them feel secure and resilient. Here are ways to create an atmosphere of support and calm for your loved ones.

Open but Age-Appropriate Conversations

In politically tense times, children and teenagers often sense that something is different, even if they don't understand the details. Having honest but age-appropriate conversations about what's happening provides clarity, reduces anxiety, and opens space for questions. For young children, simple reassurances and explanations can go a long way. For teens, who may have more awareness of current events, discussions that allow them to express their feelings and concerns help them feel heard. Remember, your kids are like little sponges—whatever you tell them is going to get absorbed and probably shared with the neighbors or a stranger at the grocery store. So keep it simple and less likely to get the family an extra 'neighborhood watch' rating.

Example: During the 2008 financial crisis, families who openly discussed changes in their finances with older children found that transparency helped build a sense of resilience. Children were more willing to support family budgeting efforts and felt less anxiety because they understood the changes.

Emphasizing Familiar Routines

Routines create a sense of normalcy. Keeping up with regular family activities—like meals, school routines, bedtime rituals, and weekend outings—can provide consistency. Small, predictable moments help reassure family members that, despite outside changes, home remains a stable environment. Find small victories every day. Even if it's just winning a round of Uno with the kids or getting everyone to the dinner table without an argument, a win is a win.

Tip: Even if you need to adjust routines slightly (like budgeting differently or changing some activities), keeping core family traditions and routines intact reinforces emotional security.

Teach Problem-Solving and Critical Thinking Skills

Encouraging family members, especially teenagers, to think critically and problem-solve can help them handle uncertainty better. Discuss hypothetical situations that could arise in your environment and invite them to brainstorm responses. This helps family members feel prepared, boosts confidence, and promotes resilience.

Example Scenario: "What would we do if there were a temporary power outage or if stores were closed for a few days?" Simple, constructive conversations that encourage practical thinking teach family members to think proactively.

Encouraging Positive Outlets for Stress Relief

Ensuring that everyone in the household has access to positive stress relief activities—such as hobbies, sports, art, or reading—can prevent stress from building up. Encourage each family member to find their own outlet for expression and relaxation.

Tip: Consider creating a designated "calm space" in your home, like a corner with cushions, books, or art supplies, where family members can retreat when they need a break.

———————————— ◆ ————————————

Case Study in Family Resilience: Life During the Great Depression

During the Great Depression, many families across the United States faced extreme financial hardship, social instability, and an uncertain future. With widespread unemployment, food shortages, and a scarcity of basic resources, families had to rely on creativity, mutual support, and emotional resilience to get by. This period offers valuable lessons in family resilience—lessons that many families today can still find relatable.

Take, for instance, the story of the Johnson family, who lived in a small town in the Midwest. The family was hit hard by the economic collapse: Mr. Johnson lost his job at the factory, and the family's savings dwindled quickly as they struggled to keep up with basic expenses. Despite these challenges, the Johnsons developed practical strategies to maintain stability and emotional support within their household.

Creating Shared Responsibilities

With the financial burden weighing heavily on the family, Mrs. Johnson established a system where each family member contributed to the household. The older children took on small jobs in town, such as delivering groceries or helping with local farms, while the younger children helped their mother with household tasks like tending to a vegetable garden and preserving food. This division of responsibilities gave each family member a purpose, and the children felt proud to contribute, which boosted morale despite the tough circumstances.

Maintaining Traditions for Stability

Although they had to cut back on expenses, the Johnsons prioritized certain family traditions to bring a sense of normalcy and joy. For instance, Friday evenings were "Family Night," where they would gather for a simple meal and play board games or listen to radio shows together. These evenings helped everyone unwind and focus on each other, reinforcing family bonds and offering a temporary escape from the daily struggles. By maintaining these rituals, the Johnsons created a steady rhythm that kept the family grounded.

Fostering Open Communication

Mr. and Mrs. Johnson recognized the importance of being transparent with their children about the family's situation. They held weekly family discussions, explaining the challenges they were facing and discussing how each family member could help. The Johnsons approached these conversations with reassurance, emphasizing that while times were tough, they would get through it together. This open communication helped ease the children's fears and made them feel like active participants in navigating the challenges.

Drawing on Community Support

The Johnsons also leaned on their community, exchanging goods and services with neighbors. They leaned on their church family where families helped each other through small acts of kindness, like sharing food or lending tools. This mutual support built a network of resilience beyond their immediate household, reminding them that they weren't alone in their struggles.

Adapting with Creativity and Resourcefulness

When money was scarce, Mrs. Johnson turned to creative solutions to make ends meet. She learned to sew clothes from scraps, repurposed old furniture, and taught her children how to cook meals using inexpensive ingredients. These adaptive skills not only sustained the family but also empowered them, teaching valuable life skills that the children carried into adulthood.

The Johnson family's resilience during the Great Depression is a testament to how mutual support, open communication, and adaptability can help families navigate hardship. While their story is set in a different era, the principles they followed—creating purpose, maintaining tradition, fostering trust, building community, and adapting creatively—remain relevant today.

For families facing instability or uncertainty, these practices offer a roadmap to staying strong, resilient, and united, no matter what challenges come their way.

———————————— ◆ ————————————

Reinforcing Long-Term Stability and Well-Being

While Chapter 4 covered financial security in depth, it's worth remembering that resilience includes having a strong foundation for both personal and family well-being. Staying focused on your long-term goals, such as savings for education, home ownership, and retirement, is vital even amid instability. These goals help create a sense of purpose and continuity, essential for mental and emotional resilience.

While resilience begins with practical preparation, it extends to cultivating a thoughtful approach to communication within the family.

Navigating Trust and Caution within the Family

In politically charged times, fostering trust within your family becomes essential, as family members may feel unsure about what they can safely discuss, especially around others outside the home. Maintaining open, non-judgmental conversations helps reassure everyone that the family unit is a safe space. However, certain precautions can help navigate this trust carefully and realistically.

Open Communication about Boundaries

Discuss the importance of family privacy and establish boundaries around sensitive topics. Encourage family members, especially teens or young adults who may be vocal about their opinions, to be mindful of where they share information or opinions. Explain the value of discretion without creating an atmosphere of fear or censorship.

Example: One family might decide to keep conversations around politics or sensitive beliefs strictly within the household, emphasizing the difference between open dialogue at home and exercising caution in public spaces or social media.

Approaching Younger Children Thoughtfully

Younger children can sometimes accidentally

share family conversations or perspectives without understanding the potential consequences. For families with young kids, fostering a sense of general safety and routine without focusing heavily on political details can be beneficial. Offer simple, reassuring explanations that help them feel safe without overwhelming them.

Caution & Reassurance for Teens & Young Adults

For teenagers and young adults, open dialogue is crucial. Encourage them to discuss their opinions and frustrations at home, providing a supportive space to voice concerns. At the same time, guide them on the practicalities of discretion, especially online. Remind them that expressing their beliefs is valuable but needs to be balanced with awareness of the current political climate.

Establishing Clear Safety Signals

In situations where political shifts lead to public or online scrutiny, establishing "safety signals" or specific phrases within the family can help if you need to communicate urgency or caution in public settings. These signals can help family members understand if they need to change the topic or disengage from a conversation when someone else becomes involved.

Setting a Safe Tone within the Family

While caution is necessary, remember to balance it with reassurance. Avoid creating an environment of fear. Instead, set a tone of preparedness and resilience, reminding family members that these are simply smart, practical measures, not reasons for paranoia. This balance will help foster a calm, united environment in which everyone feels prepared and supported.

Resilience Is a Family Affair

Protecting and strengthening personal and family resilience in uncertain times requires deliberate effort, but it also provides an invaluable sense of security and unity. From practical mental resilience techniques to thoughtful preparation and clear communication, these steps help create a sense of stability in the midst of uncertainty. Encourage family members to lean into routines, support each other, and find comfort in shared goals and simple pleasures, reminding everyone that together, you're equipped to face whatever comes next. By fostering resilience within yourself and your family, you're building the foundation for a stable, grounded life amidst uncertainty.

In the next chapter, we'll explore how to stay informed in a time of misinformation overload. You'll learn strategies to consume media responsibly, spot reliable sources, and keep a steady perspective—avoiding the trap of constant stress and paranoia.

Chapter 8
Staying Informed Without Falling Into the Abyss

These days, staying informed feels like trying to drink from a fire hose—except the water is a mix of facts, half-truths, and things you're almost certain were conjured up in someone's basement. Being informed is crucial, especially in politically turbulent times, but how do you sift through the noise without losing your sanity? Let's dive into techniques for navigating the news, accessing reliable information, and keeping your mental health intact while doing so.

How to Consume Media Responsibly in a Climate of Misinformation

In an age where everyone with an internet connection can become a broadcaster, misinformation spreads quickly. Here are practical strategies for staying informed without getting swept up by every headline or hashtag.

Filter, Don't Binge

With media constantly in our pockets, it's easy to fall into the habit of nonstop news-checking. But consuming every update only fuels anxiety. Instead, limit yourself to specific times of day to check the news. Treat it like a meal rather than a buffet—you're aiming for a balanced diet of information, not stuffing yourself with every detail.

Example: Imagine it's 7 PM, and you're winding down for the evening. Instead of scrolling endlessly, set a rule: 15 minutes for news, and then switch to something calming. Or check in during breakfast to stay updated and then avoid news for the rest of the morning. By creating boundaries, you control the flow of information rather than letting it control you.

Identify Trusted Sources (And Avoid Rabbit Holes)

Choosing trustworthy sources is essential to avoid misinformation traps. Established news organizations with a track record of credibility tend to offer a more balanced perspective. While no outlet is perfectly unbiased, well-known sources undergo more fact-checking and editorial oversight than random blogs or social media accounts.

Practical Tip: Stick to a small handful of reliable sources, ideally a mix of perspectives. Consider outlets like The Associated Press, BBC, or Reuters for straightforward reporting, then add one or two reputable analysts if you want opinions. Avoid going down rabbit holes in unverified sites or conspiracy-laden forums—these places are like quicksand for your peace of mind.

Cross-Check to Filter Out Misinformation

Even the best sources aren't immune to mistakes. Cross-checking important information is a simple way to verify facts without succumbing to paranoia. Look for the same story across multiple outlets and compare key details. If reputable sources align, you're likely on solid ground.

Example: Say you read a headline about a major political development. Before accepting it as truth, look for the story in at least two other sources. If all three describe the event similarly, it's likely credible. If there's a discrepancy, hold off on forming an opinion until more information surfaces.

Tools and Platforms for Accessing Reliable Information

In a world of misinformation, technology can also be an ally. Using a few well-chosen tools can make it easier to stay informed without being misled.

Fact-Checking Sites

Fact-checking platforms like Snopes, FactCheck. org, and PolitiFact do the heavy lifting when it comes to verifying news stories, social media posts, and even viral rumors. They can help you quickly assess whether something is true, exaggerated, or entirely fabricated.

Practical Tip: When you encounter a story that raises an eyebrow, run it through a fact-checking site before you share or react to it. These sites often break down the origins of rumors and provide clear explanations, saving you time and potential embarrassment.

Use News Aggregators Wisely

News aggregators, like Google News or Flipboard, allow you to customize feeds based on topics of interest. While they can help consolidate information, be cautious not to over-curate your sources. Variety is essential to avoid living in an echo chamber.

Practical Tip: Set up a news aggregator with a mix of mainstream sources and reputable niche outlets. Resist the urge to create narrow, hyper-focused feeds that reinforce only one perspective. Instead, aim for a healthy range of viewpoints— think of it as diversifying your information portfolio.

Apps for Digital Well-being

Platforms like Freedom, RescueTime, or your phone's built-in screen time management tools can help you track and limit your news consumption. These apps give you control over how much time you spend online and can set gentle reminders when you're nearing your self-imposed limits.

Example: Let's say you set a 30-minute limit on your news apps per day. If you start to exceed that, the app will notify you, letting you decide if you want to continue or switch to something else. Over time, these limits can help build a healthier, less reactive approach to consuming news.

Staying Vigilant Without Becoming Overwhelmed or Paranoid

The goal of staying informed is to gain insight, not anxiety. To avoid spiraling into paranoia, it's essential to stay vigilant without letting every news update become a crisis. Here are techniques to help you stay engaged without tipping into worry overload.

Focus on the Big Picture, Not Every Detail

When information is overwhelming, step back and focus on broad trends rather than isolated events. Following overarching issues instead of minutiae can help you stay informed without feeling bogged down.

Example: If political tensions are high, focus on major policy changes rather than every rumor or minor scandal. Big-picture thinking helps you maintain awareness without getting caught up in endless analysis.

Take Regular "Media Fasts"

Just like your body needs breaks, your mind needs a pause from the constant information flow. Scheduling "media fasts"—intentional breaks from news—can do wonders for your mental health and help you regain perspective.

Practical Tip: Choose a day each week or a couple of hours each day as your "media-free" time. This could be Sunday morning or every evening after dinner. Use this time to recharge without new information filtering in. When you return to the news, you'll often find your perspective refreshed.

Practice Critical Thinking (Without Losing Trust in Everyone)

In a climate where misinformation is rampant, critical thinking is essential. However, there's a fine line between healthy skepticism and outright distrust. The goal is to stay curious and analytical without assuming everything is a conspiracy.

Example: If you see a headline that seems exaggerated, instead of dismissing it outright, ask questions like: Is there credible evidence? Are multiple reliable sources reporting this? Does this fit with what I know about the issue? Critical thinking keeps you grounded without sliding into cynicism.

A Case Study in Information Resilience: The Cuban Underground News Network

During periods of restricted media access, like those seen in Cuba, citizens have relied on underground methods to access and share information. In recent years, Cubans created "el paquete" (the package)—an offline network of downloaded media, news articles, and entertainment that is distributed on USB drives and memory cards. For people without reliable internet access, this "sneakernet" provides a workaround to government-controlled media and helps citizens stay informed without risking online surveillance.

While most readers won't need to create an offline network, the example illustrates an essential point: staying informed requires creativity and adaptability, especially in restrictive environments. Whether it's using encrypted apps, offline networks, or safe channels to share information with trusted friends, you have options.

Crafting Your Own Information Strategy

In today's climate, where headlines are often designed for maximum emotional impact, having a personal strategy for consuming news is crucial. Here's how to design your own approach to information resilience.

Set Boundaries and Stick to Them

Define how much news is enough, and what types of news are essential for you. Having a plan keeps you from being overwhelmed and allows you to take in information at a sustainable pace.

Know When to Step Back

When the news gets intense, don't hesitate to take a break. These pauses prevent burnout and make it easier to re-engage with a fresh perspective.

Seek Out Solutions-Oriented News

Not all news needs to focus on what's going wrong. Sources like The Solutions Journalism Network highlight stories of positive change, showing how people are solving problems rather than just reporting them. Balancing these stories with traditional news can create a more optimistic, balanced view.

Closing Thoughts: Finding Balance in an Age of Overload

Staying informed in a time of misinformation, extreme rhetoric, and hyper-connected media can be challenging. But remember, you're in control of your media diet. You can be informed without letting the news consume your peace of mind.

By approaching media responsibly, cultivating a selective approach to information, and practicing healthy skepticism, you'll stay engaged and resilient in the face of change. Your goal isn't to know everything—it's to know what matters most and to protect your mental health along the way.

In the next chapter, we'll explore real-life case studies of people and businesses that managed not only to survive but to thrive under authoritarian regimes. By examining their successes, challenges, and strategies, we'll uncover practical lessons and takeaways that can help you build resilience, adapt wisely, and find your own path forward— even in restrictive environments. These examples provide a roadmap for navigating the complexities of autocratic systems while staying true to your values.

Chapter 9
Case Studies of Success Under Autocracy

Navigating life under autocratic rule might feel like walking through a minefield blindfolded. Yet, history has shown us that success is still possible, even under the weight of restrictive regimes. In this chapter, we'll look at how individuals and businesses have survived—and even thrived—in various autocratic settings. Each case study highlights specific strategies, lessons, and actions taken that offer powerful insights for today's readers. These stories show that resilience, adaptability, and sometimes even a bit of clever audacity can turn constraints into opportunities.

Note: The following case studies are meant to serve as examples of how people, businesses and other groups survived and thrived under autocratic regimes. They are not an endorsement or condoning of any ethical choices.

Case Study 1: Building Business Resilience in Nazi Germany

While Nazi Germany represents one of history's darkest periods, there were businesses that managed to continue, and even expand, despite oppressive government control. One prominent example is IG Farben, a German chemical and pharmaceutical conglomerate that managed to adapt its operations to meet government demands while still pursuing its own goals.

Lessons Learned:

1. Adapt Operations to Government Priorities

IG Farben's success hinged on aligning its production with the government's agenda. The company shifted focus to support industries essential to the war effort, such as chemicals for weaponry and synthetic rubber. By aligning with state priorities, the company secured government contracts and resources, maintaining production and profitability.

2. Focus on Essential Products

As authoritarian regimes often prioritize key industries (like energy, defense, or infrastructure), focusing on essential goods allowed IG Farben to avoid scrutiny while ensuring consistent demand.

Takeaway for Today:

While the ethical implications are undeniable, this example underscores the power of aligning business goals with national priorities in restrictive environments. For today's readers, especially business leaders, learning to anticipate government interests and adapting your offerings to these priorities—while maintaining personal ethics—can create avenues for stability and even growth.

Case Study 2: Personal Resilience in Soviet Russia – The Story of Aleksandr Solzhenitsyn

Aleksandr Solzhenitsyn, a Soviet dissident and Nobel Prize-winning author, is known for using his voice to challenge the brutalities of the Soviet regime. Despite facing harsh censorship, imprisonment, and exile, Solzhenitsyn found ways to share his message with the world.

Lessons Learned:

1. Master the Art of Indirect Communication

Solzhenitsyn wrote in ways that resonated with readers without directly attacking the Soviet government. By embedding his criticism in allegories and metaphors, he communicated his message to those who understood without drawing immediate censorship.

2. Build Quiet Networks of Support

Solzhenitsyn relied on networks of trusted friends and supporters to distribute his works clandestinely, showing the power of quiet alliances. These networks allowed his ideas to spread while minimizing personal risk.

Takeaway for Today:

Subtlety in messaging and careful network-building can make a powerful impact without openly confronting authority. For those navigating restrictive environments, crafting messages that convey values without overtly opposing the system can be effective, while networks of trust serve as crucial lifelines.

Case Study 3: Economic Adaptation in Modern-Day China – Alibaba's Success Story

Jack Ma, founder of Alibaba, built one of China's largest e-commerce companies by navigating the complex relationship between private enterprise and government oversight in a restrictive environment. While China operates as an authoritarian state, Ma's company flourished by learning to balance private innovation with government collaboration.

Lessons Learned:

1. Be Willing to Cooperate on Government Initiatives

Alibaba achieved success by aligning itself with national interests, working on projects that supported economic growth in line with government objectives. The company's investments in digital infrastructure and rural commerce were aligned with China's modernization goals.

2. Embrace Digital Privacy Protocols

Operating within a surveillance-heavy environment, Alibaba developed robust data security practices to protect its customers' information from government overreach, balancing compliance with privacy. Although data access is limited, this practice underscored Alibaba's commitment to customer trust.

Takeaway for Today:

For businesses, understanding where and how to collaborate with the government is essential in restrictive settings. Investing in areas that align with government interests, while ensuring ethical standards for customer data and privacy, can help balance cooperation with integrity.

Strategies for Building Resilience in Restrictive Environments

These case studies show that while authoritarian systems can stifle freedom, they also present opportunities for strategic adaptation. Here are specific strategies drawn from these examples that can help you succeed and build resilience:

Align with Core National Goals Without Compromising Integrity

When possible, find ways to adapt your personal or business goals to align with national interests. This doesn't mean abandoning your principles but finding ways to position your work or products as beneficial within the government's priorities. This alignment can provide security and reduce scrutiny, offering you room to grow.

Strengthen Trusted Networks and Build Alliances

Successful individuals in restrictive regimes often relied on a network of trusted allies. Quietly fostering connections with others who share your values provides a support system, enables discreet exchange of information, and offers a sense of community even in difficult times.

Master the Language of Indirect Communication

Just as Solzhenitsyn used allegories to communicate his ideas, those in restrictive settings today can benefit from subtle language and messaging techniques. Understanding how to communicate indirectly—whether through careful phrasing, humor, or symbolic gestures—can help you maintain authenticity while protecting yourself.

Invest in Privacy and Security

Protecting personal and financial information is essential in environments where surveillance is common. Employing digital privacy tools, protecting data, and maintaining a low profile online are crucial steps for staying resilient. As seen in Alibaba's approach, prioritizing privacy within legal constraints reinforces trust with customers and allies alike.

Develop a Flexibility Mindset

Navigating autocratic systems requires adaptability. Being ready to adjust your plans, shift focus, or even rethink certain strategies helps you remain effective in a volatile environment. Whether you're leading a business or managing personal affairs, resilience is often about embracing change gracefully and creatively.

Case Study 4: Surviving North Korea – The Resilience of the Jangmadang Markets

In North Korea, one of the most authoritarian regimes in the world, survival often means finding unofficial channels for commerce and sustenance. The Jangmadang markets—informal street markets—emerged as a response to severe shortages and government failures to provide for citizens. These markets operate outside the state economy, offering everyday goods to those unable to rely on the official system.

Lessons Learned:

1. Identify Unofficial Networks for Essential Services

The Jangmadang markets serve as a lifeline, providing goods that are unavailable through official channels. By building and using these underground systems, people are able to access food, clothing, and other necessities independently of the government.

2. Find and Protect Independent Sources of Income

Many North Koreans engage in small-scale trade or services within the Jangmadang system to supplement government-issued rations. This diversification provides some level of financial security, even in a closed economy.

Takeaway for Today:

While not directly comparable, people in restrictive environments may benefit from creating alternative channels of access—whether it's securing backup income streams, leveraging non-official networks, or maintaining personal stores of essentials. The Jangmadang markets illustrate how parallel systems of support can enable resilience when official channels are unreliable or restrictive.

Navigating Ethical Dilemmas in Business Under Autocracy

Operating under an autocratic regime poses a unique ethical landscape for business owners and professionals alike. Balancing personal integrity with professional survival is challenging, especially when faced with situations that may conflict with your values. Whether you're running a business or managing a career, here are some guidelines to help you navigate the ethical nuances:

Identify Your Non-Negotiables

Decide in advance which principles or actions you won't compromise on, regardless of external pressures. Having a clear sense of your values creates a foundation that helps you make tough decisions.

Adopt a "Minimum Compliance" Approach

Where possible, focus on meeting the bare minimum requirements for compliance without actively endorsing or promoting government initiatives that go against your values. This approach allows you to fulfill legal obligations without feeling you're compromising your ethics.

Opt for Value-Aligned Opportunities

Seek ways to align your business with sectors or areas that resonate with positive values, even within a restrictive environment. For instance, focusing on projects related to health, education, or community services allows you to make a constructive impact without direct entanglement in the regime's initiatives.

Stay Transparent with Your Team

If you're leading a business or managing a team, maintaining open and honest communication with your staff around ethical concerns helps foster a supportive environment. Encourage discussions about potential ethical dilemmas and ensure your team feels empowered to voice concerns.

Balance Profit with Principles

It's tempting to pursue financially advantageous opportunities, but when possible, evaluate the ethical cost as well. Many businesses that have survived authoritarian settings have successfully adopted a long-term view, prioritizing stability and values over short-term gains.

Practical Takeaways for Today's Readers

Each of these examples highlights strategies for operating within a restrictive system without surrendering values or losing hope. Here are some actionable takeaways:

Build Quiet Resilience Through Trusted Networks

Networks of support are invaluable. Invest time in building connections with individuals who understand and support your goals, especially those you trust implicitly. Resilience is often a group effort, and these networks can help you stay informed, grounded, and hopeful.

Practice Adaptability in Your Personal and Professional Life

Stay flexible, remain open to unexpected opportunities, and be ready to adapt to sudden changes in policy or environment. Success in restrictive regimes often requires agility, creativity, and a readiness to pivot when necessary.

Strengthen Mental and Emotional Resilience

Finally, learn to protect your mental health and emotional resilience. As these case studies show, enduring under authoritarian systems can take a toll, but by developing strategies for emotional support and maintaining a positive outlook, you're better equipped to face challenges as they come.

These stories are not simply about survival but about the spirit of resilience. By adopting strategies from those who've thrived in similar settings, you can build your own path forward—one that aligns with your values, supports your goals, and keeps you grounded in the most challenging of times.

In the next chapter, we'll dive deeper into strategies for safeguarding your digital identity and privacy—ensuring that you stay informed and connected without exposing yourself or your loved ones to unnecessary risks. From encryption tools to secure communication methods, we'll explore the steps you can take to keep your information private in an increasingly surveillance-heavy world.

Chapter 10
Securing Your Digital Identity in a Surveillance State

In a world where digital surveillance can be as pervasive as it is invisible, protecting your online identity and communications becomes crucial. Autocratic regimes often employ extensive surveillance techniques, monitoring citizens to detect dissent, control information, and sometimes even shape behavior. To navigate this landscape effectively, understanding how to secure your digital presence is as important as any other survival skill.

This chapter provides practical steps for securing your digital footprint, keeping communications private, and staying safe in a world where your every click, message, and post may be under scrutiny.

Understanding Surveillance Tactics

Surveillance in authoritarian environments can take many forms, from traditional surveillance cameras to more sophisticated methods like tracking digital communication and online behavior. Here are some common tactics used by regimes to monitor citizens:

Tracking Public Behavior

CCTV cameras, often equipped with facial recognition software, are widely used in public areas to monitor movement and activity. This data can be matched with online behaviors, creating a broader profile of an individual's actions.

Monitoring Online Communications

Internet service providers (ISPs) in autocratic countries may be required to log user activity, including websites visited and search queries. Social media platforms, too, may be pressured to provide user data or censor content.

Social Media Scrutiny

Public posts, comments, and even "likes" on social media can be monitored to gauge loyalty or detect dissent. Anything that appears contrary to the regime's narrative may raise red flags.

Interception of Private Messages

Messaging apps and email can be vulnerable, especially those that don't use end-to-end encryption. Governments may demand access to user data, making private conversations accessible to authorities.

Understanding these surveillance tactics allows

you to adopt more secure practices, reducing the risk of exposure in a monitored digital landscape.

Using Encryption Tools and Secure Platforms

One of the most effective ways to protect your communications is to use encryption. Here are essential tools and practices for secure digital communication:

Messaging Apps with End-to-End Encryption

Apps like Signal and WhatsApp use end-to-end encryption, ensuring that only the sender and receiver can read messages. Signal, in particular, is highly recommended because it minimizes data storage on its servers and has a strong reputation for privacy.

Encrypted Email Services

Traditional email services, like Gmail, may not provide the level of security you need. Consider using encrypted email providers like ProtonMail or Tutanota, which offer high levels of privacy protection and limit data tracking.

Virtual Private Networks (VPNs)

VPNs mask your IP address and encrypt your internet traffic, making it harder for authorities to trace your online activities. Choose reputable VPN services known for their security protocols and avoid free VPNs, which may log data or fail to provide reliable encryption.

Tor Browser

Tor (The Onion Router) is a privacy-focused browser that routes your connection through multiple nodes, making it difficult to track. Tor is highly secure, though it may be slower than standard browsers. Use it when privacy is paramount, but be cautious as using Tor itself may be viewed with suspicion.

Tip: Remember, even with these tools, nothing is entirely foolproof. Avoid discussing sensitive information digitally whenever possible.

Protecting Personal Devices and Data

The security of your devices—phones, laptops, and tablets—is fundamental. In restrictive regimes, authorities may attempt to access these devices physically or remotely. Here's how to protect them:

Enable Full Disk Encryption

Most modern devices allow for full disk encryption, which protects your files if the device is lost or confiscated. For example, iPhones and Android devices support encryption, as do operating systems like Windows and macOS.

Strong Passwords & Multi-Factor Authentication

Use complex passwords for all accounts, avoid reusing passwords, and enable MFA wherever possible. This adds an extra layer of security, requiring a second verification method beyond a password.

Regular Software Updates

Operating systems and apps often release updates to patch security vulnerabilities. Keeping your software updated helps reduce the risk of unauthorized access.

Secure Data Backups

Keep offline backups of important files, stored on a secure external hard drive, for instance. Avoid using cloud services for sensitive data, as these may be subject to government access requests.

Antivirus and Anti-Malware Software

Install reputable security software to detect and block spyware, which regimes may use to monitor devices. Run regular scans to detect any unusual activity or unauthorized software.

Example: In several restrictive countries, activists use burner phones—cheap, disposable phones with minimal information stored on them—to limit exposure if stopped by authorities. While this approach isn't necessary for everyone, having a "clean" device for travel or public events can be a smart precaution.

Social Media and Digital Presence Management

Managing your social media activity and digital footprint is crucial when privacy is at stake. Here's how to approach social media carefully:

Limit Public Sharing

Avoid sharing information about your beliefs,

values, or private life on social media. Keep posts neutral, and if possible, restrict visibility to friends or close contacts only.

Consider Pseudonyms or Private Accounts

In environments where expressing dissent can be risky, using pseudonyms or private accounts allows you to connect with like-minded individuals while protecting your identity. Be cautious, however, as some regimes actively monitor "anonymous" accounts.

Audit Your Friends and Followers

Be selective about who you connect with online. Review your friends and followers periodically and consider removing connections that may compromise your security.

Regularly Review Privacy Settings

Platforms frequently change privacy policies and settings, so it's essential to stay informed. Review and update privacy settings on each platform to ensure you're sharing only what you intend.

———————————— ◆ ————————————

Case Study: During certain authoritarian regimes, citizens used coded language and humor to communicate dissent subtly. By avoiding direct criticism, they were able to express views in a way that was often missed by automated censorship tools.

One prominent example of coded language and

humor being used to communicate dissent subtly comes from China, where citizens frequently use wordplay, homophones, and indirect references to discuss politically sensitive topics. In this case study, we'll look at how Chinese citizens expressed dissent in ways that often went undetected by government censors, providing an instructive model for using creativity to communicate in restrictive environments.

Case Study: "Grass Mud Horse" and the Language of Coded Dissent in China

In China, where government censorship is extensive, citizens have developed inventive ways to criticize the government indirectly without triggering automated censorship. One famous example is the use of the term "Grass Mud Horse" (草泥马 , cǎonímǎ), a fictional animal that became a symbol of resistance and dissent.

Background: The phrase "Grass Mud Horse" sounds very similar to an offensive curse in Mandarin, roughly translating to "F*** your mother" (草你妈 , càonǐmā). By replacing the offensive phrase with the seemingly innocuous term "Grass Mud Horse," citizens could share frustrations about censorship and government overreach in a way that wasn't immediately apparent to automated filters.

How It Worked: The Grass Mud Horse was presented as a mythical creature in a desert, fighting against a river crab (河蟹, héxiè), which sounds like "harmony" (和谐, héxié). "Harmony" was often used in government messaging to promote "harmonious society," but it became associated with censorship, as in "harmonizing" the internet by removing dissent. In this story, the Grass Mud Horse bravely battles the river crab, symbolizing citizens' struggle against censorship.

Memes, cartoons, and even songs were created around the Grass Mud Horse, allowing citizens to vent frustrations without explicitly stating criticism. The clever linguistic play allowed users to subtly share critiques, forming a widely understood but indirect reference to government censorship.

Why This Strategy Was Effective:

Evaded Automated Filters

Automated tools could not easily pick up on the meaning behind this wordplay, as "Grass Mud Horse" and "river crab" appear benign on their own.

Wide Popularity and Recognition

The symbolism was clear to many citizens, so the message spread widely without needing to be explicit, creating a shared "inside joke" that united people with similar views.

Adaptability

Variants of this strategy continued to evolve, with new homophones and symbols being adopted over time as previous terms were eventually flagged. The constant innovation kept the dissent fresh and less predictable.

Practical Takeaways for Today's Reader:

If you're operating in a similar environment, coded language can be a powerful tool. Words, symbols, and humor that reference popular culture, folklore, or wordplay can be understood by a community while going undetected by automated systems. While this approach requires creativity and adaptability, it can create a powerful channel for expression, solidarity, and subtle resistance.

This case study shows that even in environments with sophisticated censorship, people can find ways to communicate dissent—often with humor and creativity—allowing them to maintain a sense of community and shared values in challenging times.

———————— ◆ ————————

Communicating with Caution

When discussing sensitive topics, assume that communications could be monitored. Adopting secure communication habits helps reduce risks without falling into paranoia:

Use Code Words and Phrasing

When necessary, use code words to avoid directly mentioning sensitive topics. For instance, instead of discussing "protests," use a more neutral term like "gathering" to reduce suspicion.

In-Person Conversations for Sensitive Topics

Whenever possible, discuss sensitive issues face-to-face in secure settings. While this isn't always convenient, it's one of the most secure ways to communicate.

Practice Digital Hygiene

Regularly delete sensitive messages and files from devices, and clear browser histories. Avoid saving personal information on cloud storage that could be accessed by authorities.

Example: In some countries, citizens use humor or vague references to discuss politically sensitive topics on social media. Subtle hints, metaphors, and private messaging circles allow them to express ideas without triggering direct attention.

Safeguarding Your Mental Health in a Digitally Monitored World

The constant need to monitor your digital presence can be exhausting. Here are some strategies to protect your mental well-being while staying vigilant:

Set Boundaries for Checking Security

While staying secure is crucial, avoid constantly checking settings or accounts. Set a regular schedule to review privacy settings and device security rather than letting it become an all-consuming activity.

Digital Detox Days

Take breaks from digital communication and social media to recharge. Unplugging for a day can help reduce stress and prevent burnout.

Find a Support Network

Connect with trusted individuals who share similar concerns, either in person or through secure channels. A support network provides reassurance, allows you to share tips, and helps reduce isolation.

Tip: If you find yourself becoming overly anxious about privacy, remind yourself of the practical steps you're taking to stay secure. Small habits and routines, like regularly changing passwords and practicing digital hygiene, add up to significant security over time.

Conclusion: Building a Digital Fortress Without Losing Your Sanity

In an age where surveillance is pervasive, protecting your digital identity requires a balance of caution, vigilance, and practicality. Remember, these tools and techniques aren't about fostering paranoia—they're about empowering you to maintain privacy and security in a monitored environment.

By staying aware of surveillance tactics, using encryption tools, securing your devices, and managing your social media presence, you can create a digital fortress that provides peace of mind and practical security. While no system is entirely immune to monitoring, every step you take contributes to a more resilient, protected life online.

In the next chapter, we'll explore long-term strategies for success and security in uncertain times. From adapting your personal and professional goals to ensuring your ethical standards remain intact, we'll discuss how to build a resilient future that aligns with your values, no matter what lies ahead.

Chapter 11
Planning for Long-Term Success and Security

In a world where political climates can shift overnight, adapting for the long term is crucial. True resilience lies in building flexibility into your personal and professional plans, maintaining ethical standards as a form of "soft resistance," and, ultimately, viewing success as something more enduring than momentary gains. This chapter will explore strategies to help you navigate the future, even if that future feels uncertain. You'll learn to pivot goals without losing direction, adapt your strategies while upholding your values, and plan for a legacy that will stand the test of time. Remember, everyone has a plan until they get punched in the face. Expect a lot of punches in an autocratic regime so be ready to dodge when you plan gets knocked around.

Let's get started on setting up a long-term strategy

that empowers you to keep moving forward, no matter what comes next.

Adapting Business and Personal Goals to Survive Political Changes

When facing a shifting political landscape, the first step is to reframe how you view success and the path to achieving it. Stability, especially in restrictive environments, doesn't necessarily come from holding onto fixed goals or rigid plans. Instead, it's about staying agile, regularly reassessing your situation, and aligning your ambitions with the current reality—all while keeping sight of your core vision.

The key is finding a balance between pragmatic adjustments and a focus on long-term values. Here's how to adapt personal and business goals so that you're prepared to thrive even in a rapidly changing environment.

Reassess and Adjust Regularly

It can be tempting to put your head down and push forward on the goals you set in calmer times, but sticking to old plans during upheaval can leave you unprepared or out of touch with new realities. Just as businesses perform annual reviews to update their strategies, it's useful to do regular "check-ins" on your personal and professional objectives. By reassessing every six months—or even quarterly—you'll have a clear understanding of how recent changes impact your progress, allowing you to pivot if necessary.

Practical Tip: Set up a quarterly review with yourself (and, if applicable, with your business team). Ask questions like:

- "Is this goal still feasible given current political and economic conditions?"
- "Are there new opportunities or risks I need to consider?"
- "Do my short-term actions still align with my long-term vision?"

This process doesn't mean abandoning your aspirations but rethinking how you approach them. Treat this reassessment as a chance to reinforce your priorities and adapt, so you're ready to shift focus when needed.

Focus on Skills Over Titles

In restrictive environments, job titles or career paths you once aspired to might lose relevance or security, especially if certain sectors fall out of favor or face heavy regulation. Being the Chief Diversity Officer isn't a particularly secure position in a far-right autocratic regime. Instead of aiming for specific roles or titles, shift focus to building skills that offer flexibility and transferability across multiple fields. Adaptable skills—such as project management, digital literacy, data analysis, and strategic thinking—are valuable assets that can keep you competitive in any environment.

Practical Tip: Invest time in developing a "resilience skill set" that doesn't tie you to a specific industry. Skills like problem-solving, adaptability, and communication are universally valued and can provide stability even if your current sector is impacted by political changes.

Example: During the Cold War, many professionals in Eastern Europe found that technical skills, like engineering or IT, offered more career security than roles tied to bureaucracy or state-controlled industries. By building a foundation in versatile skills, they created job security that extended beyond shifts in the political landscape.

Leverage "Neutral" Industries

While some sectors may face tight government control, others might remain relatively stable and less influenced by political changes. Health, agriculture, and logistics, for example, often experience lower levels of interference due to their essential nature. Shifting your focus to "neutral" industries can offer a safer, more predictable path for your business or career. These sectors are generally insulated from political fluctuations, making them safer bets for long-term stability.

Practical Tip: Conduct research on industries that are less prone to state intervention. Consider options that provide a stable income while maintaining alignment with your skills and interests.

If you're exploring new fields, networking within these industries can offer valuable insights and may open doors to job opportunities with lower risks.

Case Study: Reorienting Goals During Post-WWII Reconstruction

After World War II, many German companies faced the need to quickly adapt to new government regulations under Allied occupation and subsequent economic rebuilding efforts. For example, Siemens, the technology and engineering giant, pivoted its focus to align with reconstruction needs and the demands of the time. Instead of relying solely on pre-war markets, they shifted production toward products essential to rebuilding infrastructure, such as power generation and communications. This adaptability not only ensured their survival but allowed them to emerge as a stronger, more resilient company in post-war Germany.

Lesson Learned: Companies and individuals can weather political shifts by recalibrating their goals to meet the demands of the new environment. Success isn't about holding rigidly to past ambitions; it's about understanding how to navigate present challenges while laying the groundwork for future growth.

Moving Forward

In a climate of political instability, flexibility isn't just a buzzword; it's a survival strategy. By consistently reassessing your goals, focusing on skills that transcend industries, and seeking out stable sectors, you build a framework that can adjust to even the most sudden shifts. This adaptive approach lays the groundwork for the long term, allowing you to navigate uncertainty without losing sight of the bigger picture.

Setting Up for Flexibility: The Importance of Adaptability in an Uncertain Future

When political and economic conditions shift, the ability to adapt isn't just advantageous—it's essential. Planning for flexibility means preparing for multiple possible outcomes, so you're not caught off guard by unexpected changes. Think of it as "future-proofing" your life and business, creating a foundation that can handle whatever comes next without compromising your goals.

Building Modular Plans

A modular plan is one that can be adjusted as needed without requiring a complete overhaul. Instead of a single, fixed strategy, you create smaller, adaptable components that can be reassembled or modified based on current conditions. This concept applies to both personal and professional goals.

Practical Tip: Break down your major goals into smaller, adaptable "modules." For instance, instead of one fixed business plan, create segments for different areas, like marketing, product development, and finance. If regulations change or market conditions shift, you can modify individual modules without losing the entire plan.

Example: A startup in a politically volatile country might keep separate contingency plans for different aspects of their operations, like supply chains and customer outreach. If they encounter a new regulation that affects imports, they can switch to an alternate supplier plan without completely disrupting their business flow.

Prepare Contingency Plans for Key Areas

Having a "Plan B" (or even a "Plan C") is standard advice, but in uncertain times, it's beneficial to have contingency plans for each major aspect of your life or business. These should be more specific than generic backup plans and tailored to your unique needs and risks. For instance, a contingency plan for finances might involve diversifying savings accounts across multiple financial institutions, while one for personal safety could include evacuation routes or a "go bag" with essentials.

Key Areas for Contingency Planning:

- Finances: Establish diversified savings, alternative sources of income, and access to emergency funds.

- Location: If possible, consider alternate locations for business operations or temporary residence if needed.

- Communication: Ensure you have multiple

ways to stay in touch with family, friends, and business associates.

Example: During the 1997 handover of Hong Kong from Britain to China, many Hong Kong residents and businesses prepared contingency plans due to the uncertainty of the new political regime. Some families applied for foreign citizenship as a backup, while businesses set up secondary offices in countries like Singapore. These steps provided stability and peace of mind, even though many ultimately didn't need to use them.

Developing a "Pivot Mindset"

In volatile conditions, it's helpful to cultivate a mindset that embraces change. Instead of viewing sudden shifts as setbacks, see them as opportunities to pivot. Flexibility is as much a mental skill as it is a logistical one. Adopting a "pivot mindset" means staying open to alternative paths and viewing challenges as potential doorways to new approaches.

Practical Tip: If you encounter a roadblock, train yourself to ask, "What are my other options?" instead of feeling defeated. Practicing this with minor inconveniences helps build a resilient mindset that will serve you when larger changes come.

Example: Airbnb's pivot during the COVID-19 pandemic is an example of embracing adaptability. As global travel halted, Airbnb shifted from promoting travel to focusing on "Experiences" (virtual classes and activities led by hosts) and long-term stays. This pivot allowed them to continue generating revenue during travel restrictions and demonstrated a willingness to adjust strategy based on the current reality.

Maintaining Ethical Standards as a Form of "Soft Resistance"

In authoritarian or restrictive environments, maintaining personal and business ethics is not just a personal choice—it can be a subtle, powerful form of resistance. Ethics provide a moral compass that guides actions, even when external pressures might push you toward compromise. Here, we'll explore how upholding ethical standards can serve as a stabilizing force, a method of resistance, and a long-term strategy for success.

Why Ethics Matter in Restrictive Environments

Authoritarian regimes often erode ethical norms, encouraging compliance over integrity. However, adhering to your own standards fosters a sense of agency and helps maintain self-respect, even if your voice feels silenced in other areas. Ethical consistency also builds trust with like-minded people who recognize and value integrity, creating a network of allies.

> Example: During apartheid in South Africa, some business leaders resisted discriminatory policies by refusing to comply with segregation laws in their workplaces. By treating employees equally, these leaders fostered trust and loyalty, creating an environment of mutual respect. This subtle resistance not only maintained ethical standards but also made a meaningful impact within their immediate spheres.

Balancing Ethics and Practicality

In restrictive environments, finding the line between ethical principles and practical survival is often challenging. Not every action needs to be a grand gesture of defiance; sometimes, resistance is best achieved through quiet integrity. When faced with ethical dilemmas, consider which actions genuinely compromise your values and which allow for compromise without sacrificing core beliefs.

Practical Tip: Establish "non-negotiable" ethical boundaries. Decide ahead of time which actions you will and won't take, so you're not caught off guard in moments of pressure. This might include refusing to engage in discriminatory practices, maintaining fair wages for employees, or choosing not to promote misleading information, even if those choices come with personal or professional costs.

Example: In Nazi Germany, some individuals and businesses quietly resisted by refusing to implement anti-Semitic policies within their operations. Although they faced severe risks, they drew a clear line for what they would not do, preserving their ethics even under extreme pressure. This kind of silent resistance allowed them to act with dignity and honor, even when open dissent wasn't possible.

Upholding Ethical Standards as a Long-Term Advantage

While compromising ethics may seem like a short-term solution to avoid conflict, it often comes with longer-term consequences. Maintaining your standards, even in restrictive settings, can create a reputation for integrity that benefits you in the long run. In many historical examples, individuals who adhered to ethical principles gained respect, credibility, and trust that carried forward, even after political climates changed.

Practical Tip: Think beyond the immediate future. Ask yourself, "How will I look back on this decision years from now?" Making choices that align with your long-term vision can help you avoid the pitfalls of expediency and build a legacy you're proud of.

Case Study: Quiet Ethics in the Eastern Bloc

In the Eastern Bloc during the Cold War, many academics, journalists, and professionals faced constant pressure to conform to state-approved narratives. However, some managed to uphold ethical standards in subtle ways. They maintained professional integrity by avoiding misinformation, choosing neutral language, or focusing on topics that subtly highlighted human stories without drawing the attention of censors. This approach allowed them to preserve their values while avoiding direct conflict with the regime.

Lesson Learned: Sometimes, the most impactful resistance isn't overt rebellion but a quiet commitment to doing the right thing. By maintaining ethical standards, these individuals preserved a sense of self and built a legacy of integrity, proving that success in restrictive systems doesn't have to come at the expense of one's principles.

Moving Forward

In an uncertain future, success isn't just about reaching your goals—it's about doing so in a way that aligns with who you are and what you stand for. By embracing adaptability, planning for contingencies, and upholding ethical standards, you're building a framework for success that can withstand political shifts and challenging times.

Building a Legacy of Integrity and Impact

Planning for long-term success in a politically uncertain environment isn't only about financial or professional goals; it's also about the kind of legacy you leave behind. Even in the most restrictive settings, individuals have managed to create positive, lasting impact by quietly shaping their communities and contributing to the well-being of those around them. This section is about fostering an environment where your values endure and positively influence those who come after you.

Small Acts That Make a Big Difference

Legacy doesn't always mean grand gestures. Small, consistent actions—like mentoring a younger colleague, supporting a local business, or promoting ethical practices within your team—can create a ripple effect. These acts of integrity build trust and inspire others to uphold similar values, even when public resistance isn't feasible.

Practical Tip: Identify ways you can contribute to the community or your organization in a positive, lasting manner. This might mean implementing fair hiring practices, fostering a supportive team culture, or contributing to local initiatives. Each small act becomes a building block for your personal legacy.

Example: During the apartheid era in South Africa, some business leaders implemented quiet policies to ensure fair treatment for all employees, creating workplaces where equality was upheld despite oppressive laws outside. These actions didn't overthrow the system, but they provided pockets of fairness and respect, which in turn inspired loyalty and resilience among employees.

Encouraging Others to Uphold Shared Values

When possible, use your influence to encourage others to maintain ethical standards and treat people fairly, even if quietly. In restrictive settings, many people feel isolated in their values, unsure if others feel the same way. By embodying your principles openly within safe boundaries, you create a space where like-minded individuals can feel comfortable staying true to their beliefs.

Practical Tip: Create open-door policies, host neutral discussions, or offer subtle support for initiatives that promote integrity. By doing so, you allow others to align with you without putting themselves at undue risk.

Leaving Something Positive for the Future

Long-term planning involves considering what you leave behind. Whether it's a business built on ethical practices, a community initiative, or a network of individuals who've benefitted from your guidance, thinking in terms of legacy can add meaning to your actions. Even under restrictive regimes, a positive legacy serves as a form of resistance, proving that values can endure.

Example: In Communist Poland, underground "flying universities" allowed academics and students to meet secretly and discuss banned literature, philosophy, and politics. This quiet act of resistance provided intellectual freedom for future generations, ensuring that knowledge and critical thinking survived. The people involved risked a great deal, but they left behind an invaluable legacy that helped shape Poland's future.

Practicing Long-Term Resilience: Keeping an Eye on the Future

Thriving in an uncertain environment is about maintaining hope, adaptability, and a sense of purpose that carries you forward. Long-term resilience isn't just about preparing for survival; it's about cultivating an approach to life that helps you stay grounded and hopeful, even in challenging times. Here are ways to foster resilience that can withstand the unpredictability of authoritarian environments.

Keeping a Vision for the Future

In restrictive settings, it's easy to become so focused on day-to-day survival that you lose sight of your broader goals and dreams. Maintaining a vision for the future, even if it's a quiet, personal one, is essential. This vision doesn't have to be elaborate—it might be as simple as wanting to provide a better future for your family or make a positive impact in your community. The important part is that it gives you something to strive toward beyond the immediate struggles.

Practical Tip: Create a "future vision" document where you outline your long-term goals and aspirations. Revisit it regularly, adjusting as needed, but keep it as a source of motivation. This can remind you of why you're persevering and offer hope during difficult times.

Building Physical and Mental Stamina

Resilience is both mental and physical. Cultivate habits that enhance your physical health and mental well-being, like regular exercise, good nutrition, stress management techniques, and connecting with supportive friends and family. Strong physical health can enhance your capacity to handle stress, while mental stamina allows you to stay focused on your goals without being easily derailed by the challenges of a restrictive environment.

Example: During the Soviet era, dissidents who practiced self-care, focused on health, and built personal networks often fared better under state pressure. Strong minds and bodies contributed to their ability to endure, adapt, and continue their quiet resistance.

Adopting a Growth Mindset

Viewing setbacks as learning opportunities rather than failures can help you stay flexible and adaptive. In unpredictable environments, a growth mindset—a belief that challenges can foster personal growth—helps you keep a positive outlook even during tough times. This mindset allows you to bounce back faster from setbacks, see challenges as temporary, and continuously adapt.

Practical Tip: After facing a setback, reflect on

what you learned from the experience and how you can apply that knowledge moving forward. Adopting a growth mindset trains your brain to look for solutions instead of fixating on obstacles.

Closing Thoughts: Laying the Foundation for Quiet Strength

Planning for long-term success and security in politically restrictive settings requires not just practical strategies, but a mindset rooted in resilience, adaptability, and integrity. By creating modular plans, embracing ethical standards, building a lasting legacy, and cultivating mental and physical stamina, you're setting yourself up for a life of meaning and impact—even in challenging times.

In the bonus section, we'll shift focus from quiet perseverance to the art of subtle resistance. Building on historical examples and practical strategies, we'll explore how to be a part of the resistance without drawing unwanted attention. It's possible to make a difference, even in small ways, and to stand for your values while navigating the complexities of an autocratic system. Stay tuned for practical, low-risk ways to foster change, connect with like-minded people, and lay the groundwork for a future that upholds the values you hold dear.

Bonus Section: Fight the Power

In politically restrictive environments, where open dissent can come with significant risks, it's natural to feel helpless or even isolated. But history shows us that resistance is rarely about large, dramatic gestures. Instead, it's often a collection of smaller acts, built on solidarity, courage, and quiet defiance. From the underground press in Eastern Europe to the symbolic resistance in Nazi Germany, everyday people have found ways to contribute to the fight for freedom, often in the most subtle and ingenious ways.

This section explores how people throughout history have successfully resisted authoritarian regimes, what everyday resistance can look like, and how you can stand for your values safely. You're not alone, and you don't have to risk everything to make a difference. Small actions can lead to larger movements and, ultimately, to lasting change.

Historical Resistance Movements in Authoritarian and Fascist Regimes

Throughout history, people have found ways to resist and subvert authoritarian regimes, even when open dissent seemed impossible. Studying these movements reminds us that no matter how oppressive a system becomes, there is always a way to resist—quietly, creatively, and effectively.

Key Examples:

Nazi Germany

Under Nazi rule, any form of opposition was met with severe punishment. But resistance groups, like the White Rose movement, still found ways to dissent. This small group of university students distributed leaflets criticizing Hitler's regime and urging fellow Germans to resist. Though they were eventually discovered, their courage sparked a ripple effect, inspiring others and leaving a lasting impact.

Soviet Union Dissidents

In the Soviet Union, censorship was strict, and public dissent was risky. Yet, underground literary movements flourished. Writers and intellectuals would circulate banned literature in samizdat form—hand-typed and passed secretly between trusted friends. This underground distribution kept literature alive, building networks of quiet resistance that nourished independent thought despite the state's best efforts to crush it.

South African Anti-Apartheid Movement

During apartheid, a system of racial segregation and oppression, resistance in South Africa took many forms, from large protests to quiet defiance. Black and white South Africans worked together in various ways to subvert the government's efforts to divide and control them, fostering a culture of resilience and solidarity that would eventually lead to the end of apartheid.

Takeaway:

Resistance isn't always about organizing large movements; it often starts with small, courageous actions. These movements remind us that even when individual acts seem insignificant, they can build momentum. Over time, even subtle acts of dissent contribute to the broader push for change.

Everyday People's Role in Resistance Efforts

History is filled with examples of everyday people standing up to oppressive regimes in ways that, at first glance, might seem inconsequential. But these small acts—like passing on information, wearing symbols of dissent, or gathering quietly in solidarity—created networks of support and helped keep hope alive.

Key Examples:

The White Rose Group (Nazi Germany)

Although only a handful of students, the White

Rose group took a powerful stand by distributing leaflets calling for resistance. Their message was simple but effective, stirring the conscience of Germans who felt helpless under the regime. They demonstrated that even without widespread public support, small acts of defiance can spark awareness and inspire others.

Czechoslovakia's Velvet Revolution

In 1989, peaceful protests and gatherings in Czechoslovakia led to the Velvet Revolution, resulting in the end of communist rule. What started as a student-led demonstration grew into a national movement. It shows that a single spark, carried by everyday people, can ignite a powerful wave of change.

Underground Press (Soviet Bloc)

The Soviet Bloc was known for its stringent censorship, but citizens found ways to stay informed. Underground newspapers, pamphlets, and books circulated secretly, providing uncensored news and fostering a sense of solidarity among dissidents. This quiet resistance created a shared community of values, providing hope and intellectual sustenance to those who opposed the regime.

Takeaway:

Resistance doesn't require extreme risk-taking. Small, everyday actions can contribute to a larger movement. By sharing information, attending peaceful gatherings, or quietly spreading awareness, ordinary people can play a vital role in resistance efforts.

Finding Safe Ways to Support Democratic Principles

In an era of digital surveillance and controlled media, openly supporting democratic principles can be risky. However, there are ways to show solidarity and contribute to democratic causes without exposing yourself to significant danger.

Key Strategies:

Support Independent Journalism

Independent media is often the first target of authoritarian regimes. Quietly supporting these outlets through subscriptions, donations, or simply spreading their work within trusted circles helps maintain the flow of unbiased information.

Create or Join Community Networks

Establishing informal networks with like-minded people provides both a sense of community and a practical means of resistance. These networks can act as support systems, sources of information, and channels for quiet dissent.

Engage in "Silent Solidarity"

In many places, people show subtle resistance by wearing specific colors, displaying certain symbols, or participating in coordinated acts of solidarity, like turning off lights at a specific time.

These acts create a sense of shared values without direct confrontation.

Digital Resistance

In online spaces, be mindful of digital privacy. Use secure messaging apps like Signal for sensitive conversations and consider using a VPN to access reliable news sources. These tools help protect your digital footprint and allow you to support causes while maintaining privacy.

Takeaway:

You don't have to put yourself at risk to stand for democratic principles. Supporting independent journalism, forming networks, and practicing digital privacy are ways to contribute safely. Even quiet acts of solidarity build a culture of resistance that can inspire others.

Inspiration from Notable Resistance Figures

Studying figures who resisted oppression not only provides inspiration but also shows that courage and integrity can coexist with caution and strategic action.

Key Figures:

Oskar Schindler

During the Holocaust, Schindler used his position as a businessman to protect over a thousand Jewish workers from Nazi persecution. By maintaining appearances of compliance while quietly subverting the system, he demonstrated that one person, acting within their sphere of influence, can make a significant impact.

The White Rose Group

Led by university students like Hans and Sophie Scholl, this group spread anti-Nazi leaflets across Germany. Though they knew the risks, they felt compelled to act. Their courage remains a powerful example of how, even in the darkest times, people can choose to stand up for what's right.

Vaclav Havel

A Czech playwright and dissident, Havel used his art to subtly criticize the communist government. Through plays, essays, and speeches, he kept alive the ideals of freedom and democracy. Eventually, his dedication to these values helped bring about peaceful change, and he later became president of a democratic Czechoslovakia.

Takeaway:

These figures remind us that quiet resistance, even in seemingly small acts, can create meaningful change. Each of them used their unique skills and resources to push back against oppression, proving that everyone has a role to play, regardless of their circumstances.

Balancing Resistance with Safety

While it's inspiring to think about resistance, it's essential to approach it with a balance of courage and caution. Autocratic regimes often encourage citizens to inform on each other, and surveillance is often pervasive. Being selective about where, when, and how you express dissent is key.

Key Considerations:

Avoid Overexposure

In restricted environments, avoid public displays of dissent or online statements that can be easily traced back to you. Practicing discretion and keeping certain opinions within trusted circles can help you stay safe.

Minimize Digital Footprint

Use encrypted messaging apps, avoid posting sensitive information on social media, and delete potentially incriminating messages. Digital hygiene is essential in environments where surveillance is prevalent.

Selective Trust

Be cautious about whom you trust. People close to you may not share your views, or they might feel compelled to report dissent to avoid trouble themselves. Engage in open discussions only with individuals you're sure align with your values.

Be Aware of State Surveillance Tactics

Understand the extent to which your environment may be monitored. Recognizing surveillance tools and tactics allows you to stay one step ahead without fostering paranoia.

Takeaway:

It's essential to remember that safety comes first. Resistance efforts are most effective when they're sustainable, which means balancing your desire to act with practical measures that protect yourself and your loved ones.

Concluding Thoughts

As we've seen through these examples, resistance can take many forms—from wearing symbols of dissent to supporting independent media and building trust networks within your community. No matter how small the action, each step toward preserving democratic values helps foster a resilient society that values freedom and truth.

By fostering quiet solidarity, engaging in subtle defiance, and building networks of trust, you contribute to a legacy that goes beyond individual success. This legacy can help uphold values, offer hope, and inspire future generations, even in restrictive environments. Remember, even when direct confrontation isn't possible, small actions add up, and quiet resistance can be powerful.

As we move into the final chapter, it's time to reflect on everything we've covered—the strategies, stories, and small acts of resistance that show thriving is possible, even under restrictive conditions. This journey is about more than survival; it's about finding ways to flourish without compromising who you are. In the conclusion, we'll focus on how to keep hope alive, draw strength from collective resilience, and build a life that aligns with your deepest values. Together, let's reinforce the idea that true success doesn't come from surrendering principles, but from standing firm and thriving on your own terms, no matter the political landscape.

Conclusion
Thriving on Your Terms

As we come to the close of this journey, it's time to take a deep breath and look back at what we've explored. The shifting political landscape, uncertain futures, and the challenges that accompany living under restrictive systems are, no doubt, intimidating. But if there's one thing this book has emphasized, it's this: resilience, creativity, and hope aren't just traits—they're choices, actions, and mindsets that we can nurture and carry forward. Thriving doesn't require bending to the pressures around us or surrendering our values. It's about staying grounded in who we are and using our resourcefulness to forge a path through difficult times.

Let's revisit the essence of what it means to thrive on your own terms, to stay hopeful, and to connect with the power of individual and collective resilience.

Thriving Beyond Survival: The Power of Resilience

Resilience is about more than just getting through a rough patch—it's about emerging stronger, more prepared, and more deeply aligned with what matters to you. In a world where certainty is in short supply, your resilience becomes a reliable anchor, holding you steady as you navigate the storms. Each strategy, tool, and example in this book has served to highlight that resilience isn't something reserved for extraordinary people—it's a skill we can all develop.

In the face of adversity, resilience is the quiet strength that says, I am ready for whatever comes next. It's the capacity to recover, adapt, and move forward, knowing that setbacks don't define you. Your resilience keeps you adaptable, ensures that your spirit doesn't break under pressure, and allows you to face each day with courage.

Creativity as a Form of Resistance

At every turn, we've seen how creativity can transform situations, create options where none seem to exist, and enable subtle acts of defiance. Creativity in restrictive environments isn't about painting a masterpiece—it's about using your resourcefulness to preserve what's important, to innovate solutions, and to build something meaningful despite the constraints.

Think back to those who have used art,

humor, coded language, or alternative methods of expression to navigate difficult systems. Their creativity wasn't just about producing art or protest for protest's sake—it was a way of asserting autonomy, a subtle reminder that one's inner freedom remains intact. Creativity gives you the flexibility to respond thoughtfully, to navigate the gray areas, and to push boundaries when it's safe to do so.

Every time you adapt, rethink a plan, or find a new way to connect with like-minded people, you're exercising the same creative spirit that fueled resistance movements throughout history. Use your creativity not only to survive, but to carve out small victories, uplift others, and find purpose even in challenging times.

Hope as a Strategic Tool

Hope can seem like a luxury in turbulent times. But hope, as we've explored, is far from passive. It's an active stance, a determined refusal to succumb to despair. Hope is what drives you to stay informed without spiraling into fear, to pursue your dreams even in uncertain times, and to invest in relationships and networks that bring you strength and perspective.

Hope becomes the foundation upon which we build everything else. When you foster hope—whether through small achievements, moments of reflection, or connections with others—you're not just surviving; you're giving yourself the fuel to thrive. Hope allows you to see beyond temporary challenges, helping you envision a future that aligns with your values and reminds you that, despite adversity, you have agency and the ability to shape what comes next.

Staying True: Finding Success Without Sacrificing Your Values

Navigating a restrictive environment without compromising your values can be difficult. The weight of daily pressures, subtle encouragements to conform, and the challenges of standing apart all make it seem easier to just go along with things. But, as we've seen, people throughout history and around the world have found ways to succeed and thrive without compromising who they are. They've managed to build careers, businesses, families, and communities that reflect their principles and provide them with strength.

Success on your terms means defining what matters most to you. It means identifying your boundaries and values clearly so that you can act in ways that align with them, even if it's not the easiest path. And it means embracing the belief that true success isn't just measured by financial gains or titles—it's measured by the impact you leave on those around you, the trust you earn from your network, and the knowledge that you did what was right even when it was hard.

There will be moments of frustration, of course, and times when the path seems murky. But remember, the strength to persevere comes from knowing that integrity isn't just an ideal—it's a practical approach to resilience. Standing by your ethics creates a foundation of trust and mutual respect that will serve you far into the future.

The Power of Collective Resilience and Individual Ethics

One of the most reassuring truths is that you're not alone. People across the world, throughout history, have faced challenges to their freedoms, their security, and their values. And just as they did, you can find strength by drawing on the collective resilience of others who share your commitment to freedom and integrity. When you support others, work together toward shared goals, or help build networks of trust, you're participating in a legacy of quiet defiance that has sustained generations through some of history's darkest times.

When things get tough, remember that the choices you make to uphold your values, to support others, and to contribute to a network of shared resilience matter. These choices create ripples—small but powerful—that remind others to stand strong, to act ethically, and to keep hope alive.

The path of resilience and integrity is one that honors your values, strengthens your relationships, and builds a legacy you'll be proud to leave behind. As you move forward, remember that you have the tools, the courage, and the power to thrive on your own terms. And in the end, that's the truest form of success.

Bonus Materials

1. **Quick Reference Guide to Staying Informed and Fact-Checking**

2. **Sample Coded Language Guide for Safe Communication**

3. **Personal and Family Resilience Checklist**

4. **Digital Security Basics Checklist**

5. **Guided Reflection Prompts on Integrity and Ethics**

Quick Reference Guide to Staying Informed and Fact-Checking

In a world filled with noise, misinformation, and politically charged narratives, staying accurately informed is more challenging—and more crucial—than ever. This guide provides a streamlined set of trusted resources, essential tips for identifying biased or unreliable sources, and a brief overview of tools to protect your digital privacy. Use this guide as a compass to help you navigate today's complex media landscape with confidence and security.

Trusted Media Outlets

Global News Outlets (for comprehensive, international perspectives):

- BBC News (bbc.com): Known for balanced reporting and global reach.

- Reuters (reuters.com): Offers fast, accurate news with a commitment to neutral, fact-based journalism.

- Associated Press (AP) (apnews.com): An unbiased source with extensive news coverage and verified fact-checking.

- The Economist (economist.com): Known for in-depth analysis and insights on global issues, politics, and economics.

U.S. News Outlets:

- NPR (npr.org): Offers impartial reporting and

long-form stories on current affairs, culture, and science.

- The Washington Post (washingtonpost.com): Reliable, well-researched journalism with a long-standing reputation.

- The New York Times (nytimes.com): Known for comprehensive reporting and editorial analysis.

- ProPublica (propublica.org): Investigative journalism focusing on public interest, transparency, and accountability.

Fact-Checking Resources

These organizations help verify news, social media claims, and other information:

- Snopes (snopes.com): One of the oldest and most reliable fact-checking sources for a wide range of topics.

- FactCheck.org (factcheck.org): Monitors political and policy claims in the U.S., supported by the Annenberg Public Policy Center.

- PolitiFact (politifact.com): Offers the "Truth-O-Meter" to rate claims from U.S. politicians and organizations.

- AFP Fact Check (factcheck.afp.com): Global fact-checking on political, environmental, and health-related topics.

- Reuters Fact Check (reuters.com/fact-check):

Debunks false and misleading claims on social media and in news reports.

Tip: When checking facts, compare multiple fact-checking sources to see if they report consistent information on the topic.

Identifying Misinformation and Biased Sources

Key Tips:

- Look for Credible Sources: A reliable article will often cite reputable sources, such as official reports, academic studies, and named experts. Avoid stories with vague attributions like "experts say" without clear sources.

- Check the Author: Investigate who wrote the piece. An expert in the field is more likely to present factual information than an unknown contributor with no credentials.

- Assess the Language: Biased articles often use highly emotional or inflammatory language to sway opinions. Reliable reporting tends to use neutral language and avoids sensationalism.

- Verify with Multiple Outlets: If a story appears only on one site, it's worth questioning. Stories reported widely and consistently across reputable outlets are more likely to be accurate.

- Be Cautious of Clickbait Headlines: Sensational or clickbait headlines are designed to grab attention rather than inform. Look beyond the headline to understand the full context.

Common Red Flags:

- Excessive use of all-caps, exclamation points, or sensational words like "shocking," "outrage," or "unbelievable."

- Claims that make sweeping statements with no sources.

- Stories with a call to action urging immediate response (e.g., "Share this before it's deleted!").

Digital Security and Privacy Tools

In a climate of increased surveillance and data tracking, securing your digital identity is essential. Here are practical tools and tips to help protect your privacy:

VPNs (Virtual Private Networks)

- ExpressVPN: Known for fast speeds and high privacy standards, with servers in 90+ countries.

- NordVPN: Offers double encryption and a strict no-logs policy.

- CyberGhost: User-friendly with optimized servers for streaming and torrenting.

- ProtonVPN: Created by the team behind ProtonMail, offers a high level of security and a free version.

- Surfshark: Affordable and allows unlimited devices under one subscription.

- VPN Unlimited: Affordable option with lifetime subscription option.

VPN Tip: Choose a VPN with a no-logs policy and servers in regions you trust to protect your data effectively.

Encrypted Communication Tools

- Signal: A messaging app offering end-to-end encryption, trusted for its strong privacy protections.

- ProtonMail: Encrypted email service based in Switzerland, known for its high privacy standards.

- Telegram (Secret Chats): Offers end-to-end encryption for "Secret Chats"; note that regular Telegram messages are not encrypted.

Password Managers

- LastPass: Offers secure password storage with multi-factor authentication.

- 1Password: Strong encryption, password generation, and multi-device syncing.

- Bitwarden: Open-source and budget-friendly, with a strong security track record.

Browser Extensions for Enhanced Privacy

- uBlock Origin: Blocks ads and trackers to improve privacy and browsing speed.

- Privacy Badger: Monitors and blocks invisible trackers from spying on your web browsing.

- HTTPS Everywhere: Forces websites to use HTTPS, ensuring a secure connection.

- DuckDuckGo Privacy Essentials: Includes tracker blocking and private search functionality.

Tips for Digital Hygiene:

- Enable Two-Factor Authentication (2FA): This adds an extra layer of security on sensitive accounts.

- Regularly Clear Browser History and Cookies: Prevents sites from collecting extensive data on you over time.

- Use Strong, Unique Passwords: Avoid using the same password for multiple accounts, and consider using a password generator for added security.

By using these tools and resources, you can stay informed responsibly, protect your data, and approach media with a critical eye. In a world where information is power, equipping yourself with reliable resources and digital security is essential to staying well-informed, secure, and resilient.

Sample Coded Language Guide for Safe Communication

In restrictive environments, direct communication can carry risks. Throughout history, people have developed creative ways to convey ideas without attracting unwanted attention. This guide provides an overview of subtle, coded language techniques and indirect communication methods used in repressive regimes. Whether for professional, personal, or activist purposes, these tools offer a way to communicate safely and creatively.

Using Metaphors and Allegories

Historical Example: In Soviet Russia, citizens used fairy tales and folklore to critique the state. Writers would create stories with "kings" and "dragons" representing figures of power and oppression, giving audiences an indirect way to interpret criticism.

Practical Tips:

- Pick Common Symbols: Use widely understood symbols that can easily be reinterpreted, like animals (e.g., a "wolf" for a predator) or natural phenomena (e.g., storms for upheaval).

- Craft Allegories that Echo Real Situations: Create short narratives that mirror real-life challenges. For instance, if new policies are restrictive, a story about a river slowly drying up due to a dam can imply constraints on freedom.

Example: "The forest once held a balance of power, but as the trees grew thicker, sunlight became harder to find." This could symbolize a system where centralization of power limits personal freedom.

Neutral Language with Double Meanings

Sometimes, simple words and phrases can carry layered meanings depending on context. Using this approach allows you to speak seemingly innocuous phrases that convey much more to a listener who knows the context.

Historical Example: In East Germany, citizens used words like "the weather" or "traffic" to reference government restrictions indirectly. Saying, "The weather isn't looking good" could mean new oppressive policies are on the horizon.

Practical Tips:

- Use Everyday Concepts: Refer to weather, seasons, or common activities to imply larger ideas.

- Create a "Code Key" with Trusted Contacts: Establish shared meanings for specific words and phrases so that both parties know the true implications.

Example: "It looks like heavy clouds will be hanging around all week." Among trusted contacts, this could mean that increased surveillance or police presence is expected.

Nonverbal Cues and Symbolic Objects

In many cases, physical objects or gestures can communicate messages without a single word. This approach is particularly effective in environments where even spoken language is monitored.

Historical Example: During the resistance movements in WWII, colored ribbons, flowers, and specific types of clothing or pins were used as subtle signals of resistance.

Practical Tips:

- Choose Easily Accessible Symbols: Items like certain colors, books, or small objects that can be carried or displayed unobtrusively work well.

- Agree on Meanings: Make sure that your chosen objects are clearly understood by trusted individuals but remain unremarkable to others.

Example: Wearing a certain color on a particular day, or placing an item like a single white flower on a desk, can convey messages among those in the know without arousing suspicion.

Writing "Between the Lines"

Writers and journalists in restrictive environments have long used indirect writing techniques to convey dissent. Ambiguity, suggestive language, and irony allow messages to be interpreted in multiple ways, making it harder for censors to pinpoint a single "offensive" meaning.

Historical Example: In Nazi Germany, some authors would criticize the regime by emphasizing themes like "lost freedoms" in seemingly innocent fiction or poetry.

Practical Tips:

- Use Implication Rather than Explicit Statements: Instead of saying "rights are being restricted," write something like, "The doors that once opened so freely seem heavier now."

- Lean on Humor or Sarcasm: Satirical tones can sometimes fly under the radar, offering critique without outright confrontation.

Example: "Our leaders always know what's best, don't they? I sleep better at night knowing they watch over every part of my life." In context, this line is clearly ironic, hinting at excessive state control.

Creative Examples and Code Ideas

Use of Common Proverbs or Sayings: Sometimes, an ordinary phrase can take on new meaning. For example, "Too many cooks spoil the broth" could imply overreach by government bodies in private affairs.

Subtle Critiques Through Art:

- Drawings or Photos: A simple image of a caged bird or a withering plant can represent loss of freedom or vitality. Sharing such images is often safer than direct language.

- Music and Poetry: Songs and poems can hide messages within metaphors. Consider lyrics that imply yearning for "open fields" or "wide skies" to convey a desire for freedom.

Timed Messages:

- Send Messages at Specific Times: Timing can add extra context to a message, such as sending it at a symbolic hour (e.g., 7:00 to mark a specific date or historical event).

- Arrange Meetings or Callbacks with Coded Times: Agreeing to meet "when the sun sets" could signal a late-night check-in or a conversation after curfew, for example.

Tools for Enhanced Digital Privacy and Secure Communication

In addition to coded language, using encrypted communication tools and secure platforms is critical in restrictive environments. Here's a quick overview of tools for protecting privacy:

- Signal: Provides end-to-end encryption, especially useful for text messaging and voice calls.

- ProtonMail: An encrypted email service, based in Switzerland, that ensures privacy for sensitive communication.

- Whisper Systems: Tools for encrypted

communication across multiple devices.

- VPNs: Virtual Private Networks (like NordVPN or ProtonVPN) can protect your internet browsing and make it harder for authorities to monitor activity.

In Summary

Subtle communication is both an art and a science. With a bit of creativity and discretion, it's possible to share meaningful ideas even in environments where freedom of expression is curtailed. By using indirect language, symbols, coded gestures, and secure technology, you can stay connected and share ideas in a way that respects the limitations of your environment while safeguarding your values. Remember to trust only those within your inner circle with sensitive messages and to stay vigilant for shifts in the "rules" around you—small adjustments can keep your communications safe, even under scrutiny.

Personal and Family Resilience Checklist

This checklist is designed to help you establish and maintain resilience in your daily life and home environment. Use it as a quick reference to ensure you're covering the essentials for a calm, supportive, and adaptable family setting.

Personal Resilience

1. Establish a Daily Routine

☐ Set a consistent wake-up and bedtime.

☐ Include morning and evening mindfulness or quiet reflection.

☐ Dedicate time for physical activity or exercise.

☐ Schedule breaks for relaxation, hobbies, or outdoor time.

2. Mindfulness and Stress Management

☐ Practice daily deep breathing exercises or meditation (5-10 minutes).

☐ Set media boundaries to avoid overwhelm (limit news consumption).

☐ Reflect on three things you're grateful for each day.

3. Build Skills for Flexibility

☐ Identify a few core skills to develop (e.g., problem-solving, adaptability).

☐ Set short-term goals for each skill (like practicing mindfulness, learning basic survival skills, or improving digital literacy).

☐ Use online courses or apps to support skill development.

4. Cultivate Positive Relationships

☐ Set aside time weekly to connect with trusted friends and family.

☐ Share experiences and support with like-minded people.

☐ Establish open communication with a small "inner circle."

Family Resilience

1. Establish Family Routines and Traditions

☐ Plan a consistent family meal or activity each week.

☐ Keep regular routines for children's school and bedtime.

☐ Designate time for shared downtime, such as reading or family games.

2. Create a Supportive Home Environment

☐ Set up a "calm space" for relaxation (cushions, books, calming decor).

☐ Encourage positive outlets for each family member (art, music, sports).

☐ Allow each person a daily quiet time to recharge.

3. Teach Resilience and Problem-Solving

☐ Use age-appropriate conversations to discuss current events calmly.

☐ Encourage family members to brainstorm solutions to small challenges.

☐ Role-play basic scenarios (like a power outage or supply shortage) to practice thinking proactively.

4. Foster Open and Safe Communication

☐ Establish open lines of communication for discussing concerns.

☐ Teach children and teens the importance of discretion outside the home.

☐ Create "safe words" or phrases to signal when sensitive topics should be avoided in public or online.

Mental and Emotional Well-Being

1. Prioritize Mental Health

☐ Schedule regular "mental health check-ins" with family members.

☐ Encourage expression through creative outlets (journaling, art, music).

☐ Recognize signs of stress and adjust routines to allow more downtime if needed.

2. Prepare for Unexpected Challenges

☐ Establish simple contingency plans for

emergencies (know evacuation routes, create a family communication plan).

☐ Keep a "go bag" with essential supplies.

☐ Reassess plans every few months to stay up-to-date.

3. Limit Media and Screen Time

☐ Schedule specific times to check news and avoid endless scrolling.

☐ Curate positive, uplifting media content to offset stressful news.

☐ Implement media-free zones or times at home to promote family connection.

Physical Resilience

1. Health and Fitness

☐ Incorporate daily physical activity (walking, stretching, or family sports).

☐ Keep up with regular health check-ups and screenings.

☐ Stock up on basic first-aid supplies and personal hygiene items.

2. Nutrition and Hydration

☐ Balanced meals with family-friendly recipes.

☐ Maintain a stockpile of non-perishable food items in case of emergencies.

☐ Encourage each family member to drink water throughout the day.

Practical Preparedness

1. Financial Safety Nets

☐ Diversify savings across accounts or institutions if possible.

☐ Create a simple monthly budget and track essential expenses.

☐ Keep a small amount of emergency cash in a secure location.

2. Digital Security and Privacy

☐ Use secure passwords and update them regularly.

☐ Consider a VPN for added privacy when accessing the internet.

☐ Teach family members about the importance of online caution and privacy settings.

Review and Reflect

☐ Weekly Check-In: Reflect on areas of strength and where more attention is needed.

☐ Monthly Family Meeting: Discuss any adjustments needed to routines, goals, or plans.

☐ Quarterly Goal Review: Assess personal and family goals, adapt as needed.

Remember: Resilience is a journey, not a destination. With small, consistent steps, you'll build a foundation that can weather any storm, ensuring stability, support, and calm in your family's life.

Digital Security Basics Checklist

This checklist provides simple, effective steps to help you maintain digital privacy and security, particularly useful if you're concerned about surveillance or scrutiny in restrictive environments.

1. Strong Passwords and Password Management

☐ Use Unique Passwords for Each Account

Avoid reusing passwords, especially for sensitive accounts like email, banking, and social media.

☐ Create Strong, Complex Passwords

Use at least 12 characters, mixing uppercase and lowercase letters, numbers, and symbols.

Avoid easily guessed information (like birth dates or simple words).

☐ Consider a Password Manager

Use a trusted password manager to generate and store complex passwords securely.

2. Two-Factor Authentication (2FA)

☐ Enable 2FA on Important Accounts

Set up two-factor authentication (2FA) wherever possible, particularly on email, banking, and social media accounts.

☐ Use Authenticator Apps

Instead of SMS-based 2FA, consider using authenticator apps (e.g., Google Authenticator, Authy) for added security.

3. Secure Your Devices

☐ Set Up Device Lock Screens

Use PINs, passwords, or biometric locks (fingerprint, facial recognition) on all devices.

☐ Update Software Regularly

Keep operating systems, apps, and antivirus software updated to protect against security vulnerabilities.

☐ Enable Automatic Updates

Where possible, enable automatic updates for apps and systems to ensure they're always up-to-date with the latest security patches.

☐ Use Antivirus and Anti-Malware Software

Install reputable antivirus software on your devices and run regular scans.

4. Safe Internet Practices

☐ Avoid Public Wi-Fi for Sensitive Tasks

Avoid accessing sensitive information (banking, email) on public or unsecured Wi-Fi. If you must, use a VPN.

☐ Use a Trusted VPN for Privacy

Use a VPN to encrypt your internet traffic, especially on public networks or if you need to bypass censorship.

☐ Enable HTTPS Everywhere

Ensure websites you visit start with "https://" rather than "http://" for an extra layer of encryption.

5. Email and Messaging Security

☐ Be Cautious with Links and Attachments

Avoid clicking on links or downloading attachments from unknown senders, as they may contain malware.

☐ Use Encrypted Messaging Apps

For sensitive conversations, use end-to-end encrypted messaging apps (e.g., Signal, WhatsApp, Telegram).

☐ Enable Encrypted Email if Possible

Use email services with encryption options (ProtonMail, Tutanota, etc) for additional privacy.

6. Social Media and Online Privacy

☐ Limit Personal Information Online

Avoid sharing personal details (like location, phone number, or full name) on social media.

☐ Review Privacy Settings Regularly

Check privacy settings on social media and ensure your information is shared only with trusted contacts.

☐ Be Mindful of What You Post

Avoid posting sensitive opinions or details publicly, especially in environments with increased monitoring.

7. Digital Hygiene Habits

☐ Clear Browser History and Cache Regularly

Clear your browsing history, cache, and cookies periodically to minimize digital tracking.

☐ Log Out of Accounts When Not in Use

Log out of important accounts (especially on shared devices) and avoid "Remember Me" features on sensitive sites.

☐ Delete Unnecessary Apps

Remove unused apps to minimize potential security vulnerabilities, especially apps you no longer trust.

☐ Practice Email Hygiene

Delete or archive emails with sensitive information and avoid storing sensitive documents in the cloud unless encrypted.

8. Backup and Data Recovery

☐ Create Regular Backups of Important Files

Use an external hard drive or a secure cloud service to back up important files regularly.

☐ Encrypt Backup Data if Possible

Encrypt sensitive files on backup devices to prevent unauthorized access.

☐ Store Backups in a Secure Location

Keep physical backup devices (like external drives) in a safe location.

Remember: Digital security is an ongoing practice, not a one-time task. Regularly review and update your practices to stay ahead of evolving security risks. By following this checklist, you can help protect your digital privacy and maintain control over your personal information, even in challenging environments.

Guided Reflection Prompts on Integrity & Ethics

These prompts are designed to help you clarify your personal values, establish ethical boundaries, and reflect on the legacy you wish to build. Use these questions as a guide to deepen your commitment to integrity and ethical resilience, even in uncertain times. Feel free to use these prompts as journal entries, reflecting honestly and without judgment.

1. Defining Your Core Values

What are the values that are non-negotiable for you?

List three to five values that you consider essential to who you are. Examples might include honesty, kindness, justice, independence, or loyalty.

Why do these values matter to you?

Write a few sentences for each value explaining why it's meaningful in your life.

How have these values guided your past decisions?

Reflect on specific instances where one or more of these values influenced a choice you made. How did sticking to your values shape the outcome?

2. Setting Ethical Boundaries

What actions or compromises would you find unacceptable, even under pressure?

Think about potential situations where you might

feel pressured to act against your values. Define what boundaries you wouldn't cross.

Are there areas where you might feel tempted to compromise, and why?

Explore areas where you might feel conflicted, whether due to convenience, fear, or social pressure. Identifying these areas can help you prepare for moments of ethical testing.

How can you communicate these boundaries to others, if necessary?

Reflect on how you might respectfully assert your ethical limits in a way that is firm yet considerate of others.

3. Evaluating Past Choices and Their Alignment with Your Principles

Have there been times when you compromised your values?

Reflect on any past experiences where you went against your values and how it made you feel. Consider what circumstances led to that decision.

What would you do differently in similar situations?

Think through how you might handle a similar scenario in the future, making choices that align more closely with your principles.

Have you made choices that reflect your commitment to integrity, even when it was difficult?

Describe an instance when you chose the harder path to stay true to your values. How did this choice shape your perspective on integrity?

4. Imagining Your Legacy

What kind of legacy do you want to leave behind?

Picture how you want to be remembered—by family, friends, colleagues, or your community. Describe the qualities or contributions you hope others associate with you.

How do your current actions support this vision of your legacy?

Reflect on how the way you live aligns with the impact you hope to have. What steps can you take to strengthen this alignment?

What small, consistent actions can you incorporate now to build this legacy?

Consider daily or weekly habits that reinforce your commitment to your values, such as showing kindness, practicing honesty, or standing up for fairness in your work.

5. Balancing Ethics with Practicality

What does "practical integrity" mean to you?

Think about how you define integrity in a way that allows for resilience and practicality. What would be a "practical but ethical" response in a challenging situation?

In what ways can you adapt without compromising your core principles?

Consider areas where you may need to be flexible, but ask yourself how to make necessary adjustments without losing sight of your ethical standards.

How can you stay adaptable while maintaining your sense of self?

Reflect on strategies you can use to balance adaptability with authenticity, ensuring that your response to changes respects both your goals and your integrity.

6. Affirming Your Commitment to Integrity

Why is it important to you to act with integrity, even under pressure?

Write about why living according to your values matters to you personally, especially in times of stress or change.

How will you remind yourself of your commitment when it's tested?

Consider practical reminders—like a phrase, a symbol, or a small ritual—that will help you stay centered on your values during challenging moments.

Who in your life shares or supports your commitment to ethics?

Think about people you can turn to for

encouragement or accountability. How can you support each other in staying true to your values?

7. Committing to Ongoing Growth and Reflection

How often will you revisit these reflections?

Set a plan to return to these questions periodically—monthly, quarterly, or as needed—to reassess and reaffirm your commitment to your principles.

What new questions can you ask yourself to deepen your understanding of integrity?

Personal growth is an ongoing journey. Think about additional questions or topics that might help you reflect further on your values and ethics.

How can you measure your growth over time?

Identify ways to track or celebrate your progress, such as journaling milestones or noting moments where you stayed true to your values despite external pressures.

Remember: Living with integrity isn't about being perfect. It's about making choices that align with who you truly want to be, learning from experiences, and continually reaffirming your commitment to your principles. Use this guide as a resource to navigate your journey with clarity, resilience, and a strong sense of purpose.

ABOUT THE AUTHOR

Barrett Cole is a seasoned intelligence and force protection officer with over a decade of experience in analyzing and managing global crisis situations. He has operated in more than a dozen countries, often in regions facing significant political instability and civil unrest. Having served multiple combat deployments and traveled extensively to areas impacted by conflict, Barrett brings firsthand experience in navigating high-risk environments. His expertise in crisis preparedness, including time spent in countries on the brink of revolution like Sudan in 2019, offers readers practical, actionable strategies to stay safe and resilient in uncertain times.